THE LIBRARY AND INFORMATION PROFESSIONAL'S GUIDE TO THE WORLD WIDE WEB

Alan Poulter
Department of Information and Library Studies, Loughborough University of Technology

Gwyneth Tseng
Department of Information and Library Studies, Loughborough University of Technology

Goff Sargent
Career Service, Loughborough University

LIBRARY ASSOCIATION PUBLISHING
LONDON

© Alan Poulter, Gwyneth Tseng and Goff Sargent 1999

Published by
Library Association Publishing
7 Ridgmount Street
London WC1E 7AE

Library Association Publishing is wholly owned by The Library Association.

First published 1999

British Library Cataloguing in Publication Data

A catalogue record for this book is available from the British Library.

ISBN 1-85604-227-8

Typeset in 11pt Aldine 401 and Avant Garde from authors' disks by Library Association Publishing.
Printed and made in Great Britain by Bookcraft (Bath) Ltd.

CONTENTS

PREFACE

This guide follows on from *The library and information professional's guide to the Internet* by Gwyneth Tseng, Alan Poulter and Debra Hiom (Library Association Publishing, ISBN 1-85604-221-9), which, at the time of writing is in its second edition. While the current book assumes no prior knowledge of World Wide Web, it does assume a basic knowledge of the Internet; the earlier book is recommended as the ideal source of this basic knowledge.

The intention is for this book to carry on from where the earlier book left off and to act as an introduction to the World Wide Web for librarians and information professionals, academics and students and other interested readers. It is aimed at those who wish to begin to learn how to use the World Wide Web to structure and publish information. It does not cover how to use a Web browser or how to search the World Wide Web; these topics need a book of their own.

As the earlier book, it is divided into four parts and cross-references between the parts to lead the reader. The first part, 'Fundamentals of the World Wide Web', is an introduction to the concepts, technology and application areas involved. This is the keystone of the book; it covers:

- tools and techniques for page markup, how to ensure quality in the content and design of those pages;
- advanced page markup (forms, image maps, frames, tables etc.) and its uses;
- choosing between a number of publishing models, including an externally-managed World Wide Web server and one run in-house;
- setting up and running a World Wide Web server, usage logging and security;
- publicizing a World Wide Web information resource;
- setting up a search capability for content on a World Wide Web server;
- interfacing a World Wide Web front-end with an existing or legacy back-end information system (e.g. a library automation system).

The second part, 'World Wide Web Applications in UK Libraries and Information Units', investigates current applications of the World Wide Web, in libraries (public, academic and special) and information service units in organizations engaged in the external provision of information to the public.

The third part, 'Developments in World Wide Web technology', is a more detailed look at particular areas, notably advances in fundamental World Wide Web technology, CGI and server-side scripting, and client-side programming.

Although these topics can be quite challenging and technical, coverage in this book is explanatory, rather than procedural. There are so many tools and they change so often that procedural details would be of limited use and would quickly date, due to the dynamic nature of the World Wide Web. Instead, we try to provide just enough information to encourage newcomers to World Wide Web technology to start using it successfully, and, hopefully, also provide a concise guide to those who are already publishing on the World Wide Web. The terminology is emboldened when it is first used and defined.

The final part of the book consists of a Resource Guide that can be used for more detailed and procedural information. It leads to resources on the World Wide Web itself, with pointers to software, manuals/specifications and tutorial/in-depth reference materials. This resource guide is split into three sections, each supporting one of the above parts: Fundamentals of the World Wide Web, World Wide Web Applications in UK Libraries and Information Units, and Developments in World Wide Web Technology, to match the preceding book parts. The use of resources to supplement explanatory text was well received in the *The library and information professional's guide to the Internet*. Duplication between the resources quoted in this book and the earlier one has been kept to an absolute minimum. We have tried to quote only resources that we believe to be stable and likely to be around for the foreseeable future. Some resources are cited in the preceding three parts of the book. Citations are shown by the use of italics.

PART I
Fundamentals of the World Wide Web

Contents

INTRODUCTION TO PART I

Part I introduces the concepts, technology and application areas involved in the World Wide Web. It explains the technical terms involved, outlining the history of the World Wide Web, its fundamental technologies and the steps involved in creating Web pages and building and publishing a Web site. The user is also referred to Part IV, the Resource Guide, where there is a comprehensive listing of sources of further information, tutorials, services etc. Part III continues with the theme of developments in World Wide Web technology. Part II looks at applications of World Wide Web in UK library and information units.

Chapter 1
THE CONCEPT OF THE WORLD WIDE WEB

What is the World Wide Web . . .?

The **World Wide Web** (**WWW**) is not a piece of software, like a word processing program or a spreadsheet. It is not a particular collection of information, nor is it a piece of computer hardware or networking equipment: so what is it? It started as a concept for publishing information across a computer network, which began as a small-scale project to manage and distribute scientific information across the local area network (LAN) at the European Particle Physics Laboratory (CERN). In March 1989 Tim Berners-Lee wrote a paper entitled 'Information management: a proposal', in which he stated: 'This proposal concerns the management of general information about accelerators and experiments at CERN. It discusses the problems of maintaining information about complex evolving systems and derives a solution based on a distributed hypertext system.'

. . . and what is hypertext?

Hypertext was itself a concept, but one that had been around since the days of Vannevar Bush and his Memex proposal, published in 1945 in his seminal article, 'As we may think'. Bush argued that people thought in connected strings of ideas. A hypertext system would be a practical implementation which would allow the reader to follow a chosen string of ideas or topics in published material. Following this string of topics would involve using 'jumps' or **links**, either between parts of the same document or between different documents (Figure 1.1).

A distributed hypertext system is one that has no single starting point; thus it was ideal for a network. Berners-Lee's proposed solution called this distributed hypertext system a 'Web':

> to allow a pool of information to develop which could grow and evolve with the organisation and the projects it describes. For this to be possible, the method of storage must not place its own restraints on the information. This is why a 'Web' of notes with links (like references) between them is far more useful than a fixed hierarchical system.

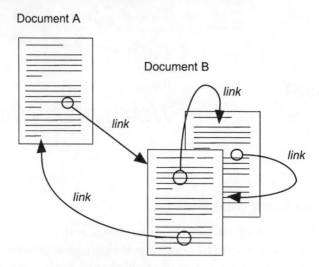

Fig. 1.1 *Diagram illustrating hypertext*

Berners-Lee went on to identify a number of practical considerations for his proposed system. It had to allow remote access across a network possibly consisting of different types of connection. Access to a variety of information sources (documents, databases etc.) in a multiplicity of forms (text, graphics etc.) was needed via different types of computer system on users' desks. Finally, the system needed to be able to expand and develop in coverage by the organic growth of linking, without the requirement for central control.

These three goals exemplify the concept that became the World Wide Web. By using a particular interface or software package, which would run on any machine, a user could access information contained in documents across a network without having to worry about the nature or source of those documents. Essentially the intention was to simplify publishing on a heterogeneous network consisting of many types of computer, network connection and software (Figure 1.2).

Thus the World Wide Web can be defined as a system allowing universal readership of documents and files over a heterogeneous network by means of hypertext links.

The history of the World Wide Web

Prior to the World Wide Web, large heterogeneous networks, like the Internet, lacked a simple method to publish and retrieve information. As the Internet grew, so did the World Wide Web, as the best means of pub-

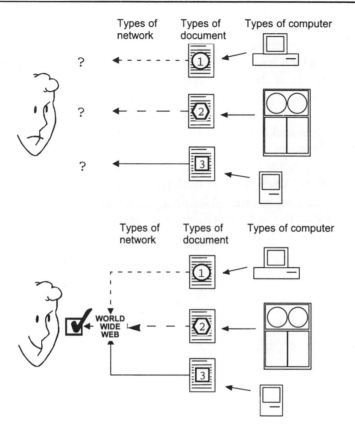

Fig. 1.2 *Computer networking with and without WWW*

lishing on the Internet. At the time of writing there are estimated to be some 200 million pages of information stored on the World Wide Web. Hypertext applications prior to the World Wide Web made little impact because they lacked a critical mass of material. The Internet provided this critical mass. The World Wide Web has become both the single most successful hypertext application to date and also the universal 'meta interface' to the enormous variety of riches on the Internet.

Having outgrown its beginnings at CERN, the development of the World Wide Web is overseen by the W3C – The World Wide Web Consortium, an industry consortium headed by the Laboratory for Computer Science at the Massachusetts Institute of Technology. The W3 Consortium seeks to promote standards for the World Wide Web. It works in conjunction with the Internet Engineering Task Force *IETF Home Page*, which is the primary organization for developing Internet standards.

Intranets

More recently, as organizations and businesses have set up their own internal networks, which have grown in complexity since their simple beginnings, the concept of the World Wide Web has been applied to creating **intranets,** in-house versions of Internet technology that are closed to outsiders. Companies have reported saving vast sums of money in making documentation available through their own intranet, compared with the costs and problems of distributing those documents internally on paper.

These developments are fully in keeping with Tim Berners-Lee's initial vision of a 'World Wide Web' as outlined above. Thus, the concept has come full circle, from its original implementation at CERN to its adoption by the global Internet and, latterly, its usage on closed-access intranets, in each case making information dissemination across a particular network easier.

Chapter 2
FUNDAMENTAL TECHNOLOGY OF THE WORLD WIDE WEB

To be implemented, Berners-Lee's vision needed a set of technological innovations. These were in three areas: a simple way of enabling computers to communicate in order to exchange files, a method of making those files universally readable, and an addressing system for locating files on a network.

World Wide Web technology itself depends on **client/server** organization. In a client/server network, one machine acts as a server and delivers services (data, applications or access to computer facilities) to one or more client machines, usually on the user's desktop. Machines can have multiple roles; that is, a server can also be a client of another server. The role (or roles) of a machine is defined by the software it is running. The functionality of a server and the ability of a client to access the facilities offered by a server are provided by distinct software packages. Thus, for a particular server function, there may be one or more software packages able to provide that function, and one or more packages able to access that function for a client. Following this model, The World Wide Web divides its functionality into two classes of software, servers and clients, although WWW clients are more commonly known as **browsers** (for example Netscape Communicator and Microsoft Internet Explorer).

The HyperText Transfer Protocol (HTTP)

In the World Wide Web, files are transferred between server and browser by means of a networking **protocol** (method of operations) known as *HTTP (HyperText Transfer Protocol)*. There are four stages to this protocol. First the client opens a connection with a server and then requests a file. The server responds by sending the file. The client then closes the connection (Figure 2.1).

In computer networking terms this protocol is very simple. The above are the only four actions involved. The HTTP protocol is **stateless;** that is, it does not record at any stage the state of a communication (such as what client is dealing with which server). The advantage of this is that there

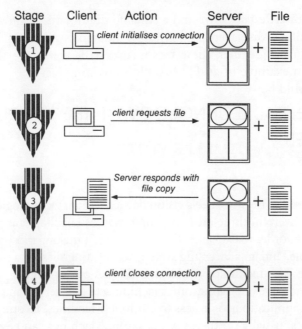

Fig. 2.1 *Client/server HTTP operation*

are no records to be kept, thus simplifying communication and avoiding problems of incorrect information about a communication. Also, the communication is not being time-controlled in any way, which is imperative in a large, complex network in which responses cannot be guaranteed.

HyperText Markup Language (HTML)

HTTP is the delivery mechanism for files using the World Wide Web. The item delivered is a file in **HTML** (HyperText Markup Language) format. HTML is a simplified derivative of **SGML** (Standard Generalized Markup Language). A **markup language** is a system for describing the layout and format of information on a page or a screen.

HTML consists of **markup tags**, usually organized in pairs (i.e. <*start tag x*> and </*end tag x*>, although some tags do not have an 'end' tag pairing. Using a start without a corresponding end tag may cause a visible error, as will tags that are formed incorrectly. Tags fall into two general groups: they either affect the display and structure of a document or they are necessary to allow a browser to recognize a file as containing HTML tags. This latter group will be dealt with first.

Each HTML file starts and ends with a pair of tags showing that it is an HTML document. Within the file, tags delimit a **header**, containing information about the content, and a **body**, for the content itself. In the header, a pair of **title** tags surround a suitable title for the content of the file, which will be displayed as a window title in a graphical browser (Figure 2.2). Taken together, these tags form a basic **template** for every HTML file. An example of an HTML file, consisting just of basic structuring tags, would be:

```
<HTML>
<HEAD>
<TITLE>Example HTML page</TITLE>
</HEAD>
<BODY>
This is an example HTML page.
</BODY>
</HTML>
```

HTML is not intended to be a comprehensive page layout system. Instead, it can describe a document by indicating headings, paragraphs, emphasis and so forth (Figure 2.3). Tags can also indicate where hypertext links occur. There are many things that cannot be done easily with HTML when structuring a document, for example, putting text into columns. A small subset of content tags, for features like headings, paragraphs, text styles and lists, will serve as the basis for many pages. In fact, they can be all the tags that are required. Adding some basic content tags for a heading and a paragraph gives:

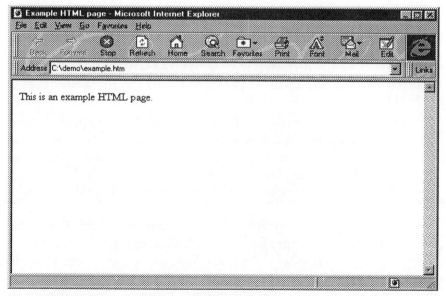

Fig. 2.2 *Screen dump of the basic HTML page*

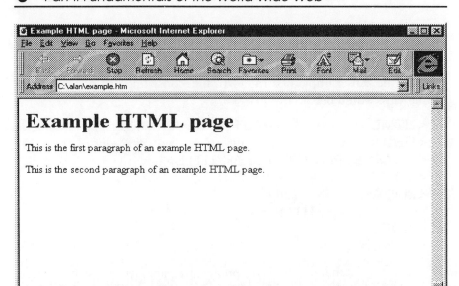

Fig. 2.3 *Screen dump of the basic HTML page with content*

```
<HTML>
<HEAD>
<TITLE>Example HTML page</TITLE>
</HEAD>
<BODY>
<H1>Example HTML page</H1>
This is the first paragraph of an example HTML page.<P>
This is the second paragraph of an example HTML page.
</BODY>
</HTML>
```

There are several versions of the HTML standard. The earliest could handle only textual content, but later versions have included the ability to tag non-textual content (graphics etc.) and also much wider abilities to structure and display content. The W3 Consortium is the body that sets and develops the HTML standard. The latest version is HTML 4.0 (April 1998).

All HTML tags are in **ASCII (American Standard Code for Information Interchange)** format, which all computers can understand. These are easy to mix in with content, which, in the case of text, is also in ASCII format. When a browser receives an HTML file, it uses the tags to display the content of the file. The display of content is dependent upon the capabilities of the browser and the computer on which it is running. Thus the same HTML file may look different when viewed by different browsers on different computers, but its content will remain the same.

Uniform Resource Locators (URLs)

With HTTP providing delivery and HTML providing display of content, there only remains a need to identify and retrieve, by means of links, files on the network. An identification and addressing mechanism is provided for the World Wide Web by the **URL** (Uniform Resource Locator). A URL consists of five elements:

protocol://domain:port/path/filename

Protocol is typically HTTP but most browsers can also handle other Internet retrieval protocols, for example FTP (File Transfer Protocol), NNTP (Network News Transfer Protocol) etc. **Domain** is a name (or equivalent numeric code) that uniquely identifies a computer on a network. **Port** is rarely seen as it specifies a special connection into the server. **Path** is a list of directories, beginning in the **root directory** (the initial directory) that the World Wide Web server running on a computer is using for storing files. Finally, **filename** is the name of a file in HTML format. If the final element of a URL is a '/' and not a file name, then the default file name can typically be assumed to be 'index.html' (although this can be changed to other names by local settings). Links in HTML are expressed as URLs and tagged so that a browser can identify them as a link.

In the following example:

http://www.uni.ac.uk/staff/jbloggs/

'http' is the protocol, 'www.uni.ac.uk' the domain, and the remainder is the path ('staff' is a directory in the root directory, 'jbloggs' a directory in the 'staff' directory) (Figure 2.4). Since no name of the file to be retrieved is given, it is assumed to be index.html.

In HTML, links are expressed in the following form, essentially as a URL for the destination as a hypertext reference (HREF) followed by some text that will appear underlined in blue in a browser, indicating that a clickable link is present:

<A HREF=" http://www.uni.ac.uk/staff/jbloggs/">Click here to go to the staff page for J.Bloggs </A>

For more information see Part III: 'Fundamental Web technology' (Chapter 8).

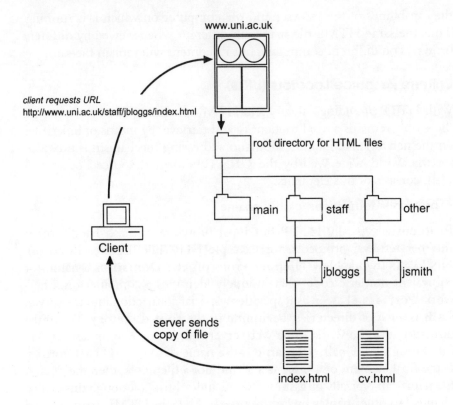

Fig. 2.4 *File retrieval using the URL http://www.uni.ac.uk/staff/jbloggs/*

Chapter 3
CREATING WEB PAGES

Page creation tools

A file in HTML format available for retrieval by a browser on a World Wide Web server is known as a **page**. A **document** may be contained in one page, or consist of a number of linked pages. The collection of pages stored on a particular server is known as a **site** (or **Web site**).

Web pages are not built online, using a 'live' server. They are typically created on a personal computer, saved to the hard disk and viewed from the hard disk **offline** by a browser.

There are a number of ways to create Web pages. Once the basic HTML tags are understood, one way of creating a page is to use a text editor or a word processor (taking care to save it as ASCII text) and simply enter tags around the content. This way might be slow and demands a good knowledge of HTML but it does give the creator most control over each page.

Another way to create a page is to use an **HTML editor**. Basic HTML editors are no more than text editors, with HTML tags available from menu options. These are slightly faster to use because they remove the need to type in tags. However, a knowledge of HTML and its facilities is still required. Some HTML editors offer '**wizards**', which are routines for building a page for a particular purpose, for example, a **home page** (for recording information about yourself).

Advanced HTML editors, sometimes known as **Web page creation software**, are more like standard word processors in that they enable content etc. to be entered and laid out, with no need for the addition of tags, which is done automatically by the package itself. Pages are fast to build in this way but the creator has no control over the tags as such.

These tools are only for creating new documents. Existing documents can be converted into HTML by special **HTML converter** software. While many documents can be converted automatically in this way, they will still require visual inspection with a browser and more often than not, corrections made to their HTML tags. Finally some word processors have the ability to save a document in HTML format. This ability may require special extra 'add-on' software for the word processor.

No one page creation method is right for all occasions. Perhaps the best approach is to have to hand both a preferred HTML editor and a Web page creation tool. These should be supplemented by a knowledge of HTML, since it is unwise to have no understanding of how HTML works. For example, some problems can be easy to fix using a simple text editor to change HTML tags, but not so easy with more sophisticated page creation software.

Page layout and structure

Some standards for page appearance are universal. Pages should have meaningful titles (not just 'Welcome page', but 'Organization X: Welcome page'), a clear purpose and appropriate content, properly organized under headings. Big unbroken blocks of text should be avoided, as should the overuse of styles like bold or italics. Just as for word processed documents, text on Web pages should be spell-checked and grammatically correct.

It is good practice to allow space for the URL of the page to be on the page itself, along with the name and e-mail address of the person responsible for the page and the date the page was last updated. Each page should be considered a self-contained entity (they can be printed or browsed individually) so each one needs these identification and authorship details.

Many printed documents use columns in some way to lay out text and graphics. This can be emulated in HTML by using **tables**. Originally intended as a way of displaying tabular information, such as statistical data, tables can be pressed into service as a layout device. Essentially, the grid of the table is not shown, but rather its rectangular elements are used to contain text and images (Figure 3.1).

It is possible to subdivide the browser window using **frames.** This facility is used for holding in view information that may be relevant across pages on a Web site. For example, a menu or page index can be held in one small frame, while the main frame views pages (Figure 3.2). It should be noted that frames have their detractors. Anything that can be done with a frame can be achieved by using more basic HTML facilities (e.g. a list of words on a line, each of which is a link, can function like a menu bar).

Cascading style sheets (CSS) provide a simple means of styling HTML pages, allowing control of visual characteristics such as fonts, margins, line spacing, colours etc. These can be achieved on the latest browsers, but they degrade gracefully when used with older browsers. Style sheets offer total control over every aspect of a Web page: specific font sizes, types, and colours can be set section by section or even element by element on a page.

14

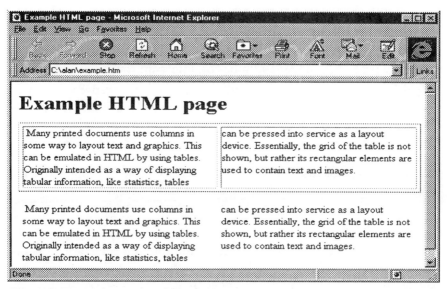

Fig. 3.1 *Screen dump of a tabular Web page*

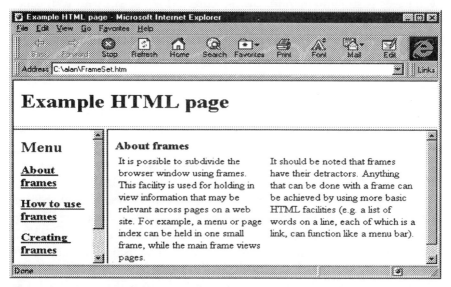

Fig. 3.2 *Screen dump of a Web page with frames*

Checking Web pages

Whichever method of Web page creation is used, it is vital that the appearance of all the pages is checked by browsing them. Once changes are made and saved to disk, the page must be reloaded in the browser to see the effect of the changes, otherwise the 'old' copy in the browser **cache** (a temporary disk store for Web pages viewed in the current session) will be shown. This may prompt further editing, and so on. It is also prudent to see how a page looks under a number of different browsers, because each one displays certain HTML elements in slightly different ways.

Messages exhorting the user to use a particular version of a specific browser, or to change their viewing window to a certain size, or similar, should be avoided. In fact, it is worth trying to view pages via as many browsers on different computer platforms as possible, to be forewarned of any potential problems. When writing pages, assume nothing about the cultural background of the possible users of those pages.

Learning HTML

Learning HTML may seem somewhat daunting, but there are an enormous number of HTML tutorials/Web page creation guides and reference sources available on the Internet. *Writing for the Web – a Primer for Librarians* and *The Bare Bones Guide to HTML* are recommended. Since the layout of Web pages is still an emerging art, be sure to look at as many Web pages created by other people as possible, both for design ideas and for the HTML markup they use. The latter can be viewed using a browser to 'view source'.

Style guides

Learning HTML is, however, not the whole story; one must also have an appreciation of how it can be used to structure a page effectively. There are a plethora of style guides available on the Internet containing plenty of advice, some of it conflicting, on what makes a Web page look good. *Yale C/AIM Style Guide* is the best starting point.

There are essentially two approaches to the finer points of Web page appearance and layout. One recognizes that HTML is not intended to enable the faithful reproduction of traditional paper page layouts on Web pages and that it constrains designs accordingly. The second approach does not accept the limitations of HTML and works around these to use traditional printed page layouts as the basis for Web pages. Each approach has its advantages and drawbacks. The first stays true to the intent of HTML but these pages might not look as good as those produced by the second approach. The latter can lead to page creators forgetting the 'universal access' goal of the World Wide Web, with the production of monstrosities such as Web pages consisting only of graphics, with no explanatory text.

Finally, a sensible approach to aim for is a common look and feel for individual pages. Style may be constrained by a **template**, which lays down elements that have to be present on a page (e.g. an organization's logo). Templates are especially useful when Web page creation is done by a team or numerous individuals rather than by just one person, because they serve to ensure a house style for all pages. The variety of media and functions that can be delivered via a Web page almost necessitate a team effort. **Webmaster** is the typical name for the person who either oversees or produces pages for a Web site.

Web page graphics

The most basic adornment to a textual Web page is graphics. HTML tags can be used to include images in Web pages alongside text, using the <IMG SRC="graphicfilename"> tag. These images are known as **inline graphics**. Images can also be displayed on their own in a browser window. The rationale for doing this is that the image needs a full screen view. Such images are retrieved by following a link. Against this link should be a description of the image or a **thumbnail image** (reduced size version) of it. The size of the linked image should also be given, to enable loading time to be estimated.

Images can function either as icons or as page adornments, or they can contain information in their own right (e.g. a diagram). There are libraries of both icons and **clip art** (pictures in the public domain) available on the Internet (see *Clip Art Searcher*). If images need creating or editing, there are many shareware or freeware **image editors** (also known as **paint packages**) available for download. 'Photoshop' is the standard commercial package. Images can also be **scanned** (converted into digital format from a photograph or printed original) by a scanner or captured using a **digital camera** (a camera that stores photographs in digital form and not on film).

However images are obtained, they may need converting into one of two main **graphics file formats** that are used on the World Wide Web, **GIF (Graphics Interchange Format)** or **JPEG (Joint Photographic Experts Group).** Either special image converter software, or most image editors, will do this **conversion** (usually by saving a graphics file in a chosen format). JPEG is best for photographic images while GIF is best for line-art images, such as icons and logos. It is unwise to convert from GIF to JPEG, or to edit an image and repeatedly save it in JPEG. This is because the quality of the image will suffer.

When using inline graphics, if including an image that is larger than a typical icon, it is advisable to indicate its size by means of width and height attributes in the HTML image tag, so that the browser can format the entire page without waiting for that image to start downloading. Images

17

should be kept to a minimum size, so that they load as quickly as possible. It is possible to keep image file sizes small by minimizing the number of colours used in the graphic; 256 colours is the maximum that should be used, but 16 can be enough. Logos may need even fewer colours. The *Bandwidth Conservation Society* gives good advice on minimizing the size of graphics files.

When a browser loads a page, **interlaced GIFs** appear at first. They have poor resolution, which improves while the entire image arrives. This is intended to give an impression of what the image will look like while waiting for the rest. Interlaced GIFs can be created by saving GIFs in interlaced format. **Animated GIFs** cycle repeatedly through a short animated scene. While animated GIFs can have serious uses (e.g. showing the effects of mixing certain chemicals) they can also be irritating, so use them sparingly! Special software is required to create them.

Transparent GIFs are images that blend in smoothly with whatever background colour has been chosen. This is done by assigning one colour in the GIF to be transparent so that it will be replaced by the background colour. For information about progressive JPEGs (equivalent to interlaced GIFs) see the *JPEG FAQ*. *MediaBuilder* is a great source for all kinds of image manipulation tips.

Beware of overusing images; not all users have a graphical browser and many turn graphics off voluntarily to save download time. Make sure any page with graphics is usable without having to view the images it contains.

Text and background colours

It is not necessary to use graphics to add colour to a Web page. The background, text, links etc. on a page can be given specific colours by using attributes of the BODY tag and numbers for colours. Colours are expressed by means of a six-digit hexadecimal number (ranging from 00 to FF), with pairs of digits representing intensities of red, green and blue. See *RGBtoHex* for the colours that various numbers produce. Note that background and text colours ought to be chosen with caution, bearing legibility in mind. Individual browsers may have different interpretations of the same colour, which can lead to some strange looking Web pages!

Finally, rather than use a background colour, an image may be used as a **background graphic**, by specifying it following a BODY tag. Background graphics are created in exactly the same way as standard graphics. Libraries of background graphics are available for free download.

Sound and video on Web pages

Whether Web page graphics are in GIF or JPEG format, any browser running on a computer with a graphical user interface (like Windows) will be able to display them. Unfortunately, no such universal acceptability of formats exists for sound or video files. There are currently a plethora of sound and video file formats available on the Internet. Not all formats are supported by all browsers. Although free **plug-ins** (an extra internal browser function) or **helpers** (a separate piece of software activated by a browser) are available to play a sound or video file format, the individual user accessing a particular sound or video file may not have the correct software loaded. The last resort with a sound or video file is for a browser to save it to disk, but this may be a waste of disk space if the stored file cannot be played on that computer

Therefore a difficult decision that has to be made when providing a sound or video file is what format it should be in. **WAV**, **AU** and **AIF** are the commonest sound file formats, while **AVI**, **MPEG** and **Quicktime** are the commonest ones for video. There are shareware and freeware tools available for creating, editing and converting between different sound or video file formats, as well as commercial packages. There are also libraries of sound and video clips available for download. Finally, there are a wide range of devices for capturing sound and video in digital form.

Like graphics, Web pages may have links to sound and video files or the files may be **embedded** in Web pages, so that they are downloaded at the same time as the page itself. Unlike graphics, once retrieved by either method, a sound or video file is sent to the browser, which will then either play the sound or video file, or pass it to an appropriate plug-in or helper, or save it to disk. Even more so than with images, sound and video files should be used sparingly because their size makes them very slow for most users to download over the Internet. Alongside the link to any sound or video file should be an indication of its file size in megabytes, to help users to decide whether to download it or not. Embedding sound and video files can be regarded as a waste of bandwidth if large files are sent to users who are unable to play them.

As well as sound and video files, there are also special formats for distributing multimedia presentations, combining still graphics, animation, sound and video, over the Internet. Perhaps the most influential of these is Shockwave from *Macromedia*. As with sound and video files, there is still a large file to transfer to the user's browser and the need for a special plug-in or helper to play the multimedia presentation when it has been downloaded.

One way of reducing the necessity of downloading large sound or video files in their entirety is to **stream** their content to users (i.e. send a continuous flow of data for sound or video). Again, there are a number of formats for streaming, but the most popular seems to be Realplayer from *RealNetworks*.

Synchronized Multimedia Integration Language (SMIL) is a newly-defined tagged language which is intended to be used for multimedia presentations involving timed sequences. It is bandwidth friendly, yet adaptable to streaming applications. Finally, **VRML (Virtual Reality Modelling Language)** is another tagged language, now into its second version, but one intended for creating three-dimensional worlds.

Data files and software on Web pages

Data files (files storing data in a particular format required by a piece of software, such as a word processor or a spreadsheet) and software files themselves, can be linked to Web pages. Normally, data files will be saved straight to disk when downloaded, but a browser can be configured to launch either the software they require or, depending on availability, a **viewer**, a cut-down version of the necessary software, which cannot make changes to the file. Viewers for many popular data file formats are available for download from the Internet. Software needs a particular type of computer and operating system in which to function. These requirements should be specified alongside the link to enable users to know whether their computer can run the downloadable software.

In order to reduce storage, data files and software are normally stored in **compressed** form, using one of a number of different compression packages. Thus a downloaded file in compressed form is unusable until it is decompressed. For each file it is vital to indicate what compression software (if any) was used; this can normally be done by using an accepted file extension showing the compression software used. *Common Internet File Formats* is a good source for linking these file extensions to the compression software that created them. Most compression software is available as freeware or shareware and is downloadable.

An accurate file size in bytes should also be given, to aid in judging download time and in checking the completeness of the download. Files should be named with eight-character file names and three-character extensions, all using lower case alphabetic characters, so as to cause no file handling problems, whatever type of computer is used to download them. Finally, if possible, individual files should be compressed to no larger than 1.4 megabytes, the capacity of a floppy disk. Files larger than this take a long time to download (which may mean that the download will abort) and are not transportable on floppy disk when downloaded, due to their size.

Although all this sounds quite daunting, Web pages are an excellent medium for distributing software. Browsers can be configured to call appropriate decompression software for downloaded files. Making data files for standard software packages like word processors, spreadsheets etc. accessible via an intranet avoids having to convert those data files into HTML, yet makes them easily available.

Interactive Web pages

An interactive Web page is one that produces some particular response to user activities. The earliest method of making Web pages interactive was to use a **form,** a Web page containing a data entry screen built in HTML, which could be filled in by a user and then activated by an onscreen SUB-MIT button, again created in HTML. For example, users could be asked to fill in their name and address on a form to register for a service or to send in a comment. The data gathered from the user could then be passed back to a Web server for processing. All Web servers have a **CGI (Common Gateway Interface)** facility to call up software resident on the same computer as the server, but external to the server itself, to process the data from the form. Thus the use of CGI by the server is similar to the use of helpers and plug-ins by a browser. The software called up by the CGI processes the user's data and may return results (or just a confirmation of processing) back to the user in the form of a Web page (Figure 3.3).

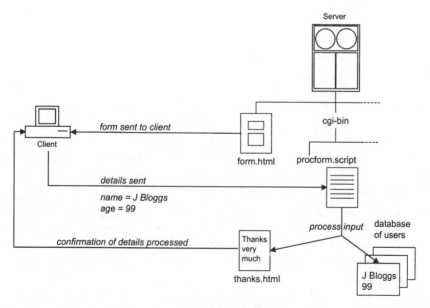

Fig. 3.3 *Diagram showing form processing by a CGI script*

Processing data from forms is usually done by **scripts** (simple programs) written in a programming language suitable for the task. Form processing mostly involves reading in textual data, processing it and returning processed data and/or a response as a Web page, which itself is built from text tags. The majority of CGI scripts are written in a computer language called **PERL** (Practical Extraction and Reporting Language) which is eminently suited to the task, being able to process text quickly and efficiently.

Another use of the CGI facility is to invoke a local search program to enable word searching of Web pages. Adding a search capability for an individual Web site can be invaluable for users, as it can offset the difficulty of finding information by browsing links. Local search engine software is available, both freely and commercially (see the excellent *Site Search Tools* for a guide to this software). The better external Web space providers are likely to provide a search capability.

A third common use of CGI is to allow access via the Web existing mainframe- or minicomputer-based software applications, sometimes known as **legacy** applications. To interface a World Wide Web server with an existing or legacy information system (e.g. a stock control system or an online public access catalogue) one needs either to write a script to access the legacy system, presenting data from it in HTML, or use vendor-supplied tools for the task. Apart from CGI, there are many proprietary methods available for linking a server to other applications, which go under the generic label of **middleware**, since they exist only to link servers with other applications. The *Intranet Software Catalog* has links to a good selection of middleware packages. For more information see Part III: 'CGI and server-side scripting' (Chapter 9).

Interactivity as described so far, is dependent on access to a CGI facility on a server. Without this access, data cannot be processed. Without CGI, for example, data from a form could only be converted to an e-mail and sent to a human operator for processing. However, another approach is to create software capable of processing user responses, but to run that software in the user's browser and not via CGI on a server. **Java** is perhaps the best known of a number of ways for software applications to be delivered via World Wide Web. A Java program is embedded in a Web page. When a user views that Web page, the Java program is automatically loaded and executed by that user's browser. Data and the software to process it can be delivered in the form of so-called '**applets**' (little applications), but the browser needs to be 'Java enabled' to be able to run them (Figure 3.4).

There are performance issues because Java applets may be slower to run than local software. There are also possible security problems. Java applets are prevented from harming the local machine that the browser is running

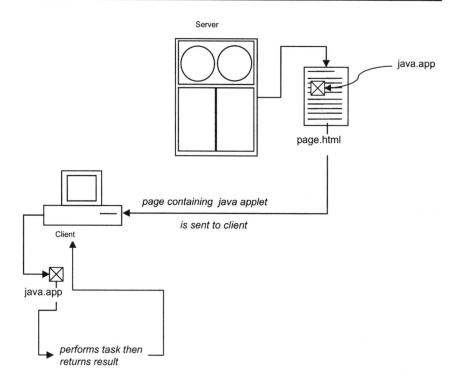

Fig. 3.4 *Diagram showing how a Java applet works*

on by not being allowed access to the local file system.

There are a number of alternatives to Java, although it stands out from the others because it attempts to be independent both of browser and machine (it will run in any 'Java enabled' browser on any machine), while other similar programming languages may not be so broadly based, for example, **Javascript** (from Netscape Corporation) or **ActiveX** (from Microsoft). The latter requires a machine to be running Windows 95 or NT to function. For more information see Part III: 'Client-side programming' (Chapter 9)

Chapter 4
DESIGNING WEB SITES

Basic design

The basic goal of information provision via the World Wide Web is to understand the needs of users and design a Web site around these needs. Web site design is a vital activity that should precede the creation of actual pages, since each page should have a specific purpose and place in the site. Most Web sites consist of many pages, since one page is not usually sufficient to carry all the information required. An exception might be an individual's home page, in that the information requirements are basic (work history, educational qualifications etc).

More typically, in the case of an organization providing information about its departments or the services it offers etc., separate pages might be required to hold information about each particular department or service. The problem of designing a Web site revolves around the problem of allocating information content to pages and then forming those pages into a browsable entity (the Web site), which ought to have a logical structure.

It is a good idea to try to use a diagram as a planning aid to show links between pages. The standard practice is to structure a Web site so that there is an **index page** (or **main** or **root** page), which leads hierarchically to all pages that make up the site. Each of these pages should contain a link back to the index page and may contain links to other pages. An alternative is to have a **site map** page, which illustrates, usually by means of a diagram, the main sections and linkages between them. The site map is reached by a prominent link on all pages.

The temptation to link each page to every other page should be avoided. Try to ensure the minimum number of links on each page; they should be just to other pages that contain related content. Be as consistent as possible in the number and function of links on each page. Do not bury information down a long path of links. A rule of thumb is that every item on a site should be reachable by following no more than two links, one from the index page to a second page and then a link from the second page to the desired item.

For a hypothetical company, the index page would list its departments and services, and contain links to a page for each one. Each departmental page would contain links to pages for the other departments and to pages for service(s) offered by that department. Each service page would link to the other service pages and to each department that offers that service. Each departmental and service page would link back to the index page (Figure 4.1).

Many Web sites need to contain documents (plans, manuals, reports etc). Individual documents are typically structured either as one long page with links to each section from a contents list at the top, or by each section being on a separate page, with a contents page linking to all sections and each section linking to its immediately preceding and succeeding sections. The length of the document determines which design strategy to use, with only short documents being suitable for the former.

If absolute fidelity of representation of paper documents on the Web is required, another option is to use **PDF (Portable Document Format)**, a replacement for HTML. The only difficulty with this is that special (free) reader software needs to be added to a browser to enable the viewing of PDF files.

No Web site will be static because information will be added, amended and removed over time. If the initial design was correct, then there should be no need to reorganize the basic linking and structure of the site. However, expansion in terms of adding completely new pages and deleting redundant pages (if any) must be allowed for and should grow naturally out of the initial design. Although the basic structure of a Web site

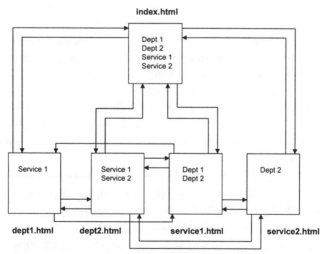

Fig. 4.1 *Diagram showing good linking strategy for the example hypothetical company Web site*

ought not to change over time, the information on individual pages certainly will change and some provision must be made to make users aware of new or updated information. The best technique is a list of **update** pages, each of which is dated and contains links to the new or changed information added on that date. This allows users to scan back for any new information of interest that they may have missed. If updates are made periodically (weekly, monthly etc. as appropriate) then users will learn to expect them and will adjust their browsing accordingly.

The design model suggested above cannot cover every Web application. A good practice is to browse Web sites that are similar to the application area being developed, and try to ascertain their structure of pages and links in order to see other models in operation. Always remember that a good Web site will map its linking and page structure neatly on to the information its users want from it; a bad one will not. Again, there are many sites giving good advice on design; those recommended are *Usable Web* and *The Alertbox: Current Issues in Web Usability.*

File structures and links

Once you have a clear design for your Web site in terms of content, pages and links, then the connecting links can be built, for which Web pages must be stored on disk so that links can point to particular pages by using their file name.

Web pages are computer files and, as such, need to be stored on disk. It is inadvisable to store all the pages in one directory, as the resulting clutter can be hard to understand and maintain. It is recommended that a directory structure should be used to store pages and that the pages are grouped in directories by similarities in their content. The index page should go in the root directory, and others into subdirectories named for the subject of the pages they contain. If the use of common images is made (e.g. a logo), it is a good idea to store these in a directory reserved just for images. For the hypothetical organization described previously, underneath the index page in its root directory would be two subdirectories, one called 'departments', the other 'services'. Pages comprising a document should go into a separate directory (Figure 4.2).

Files for pages should be named so that their content is apparent. It is best to use eight-character file names and three-character extensions because this naming convention is the lowest common denominator that all computer systems will accept. For the same reason, file names for pages should contain only alphabetic characters, which should all be in lower case. The extension '.htm' denotes a file containing HTML and is used on DOS/Windows systems. Files created in other systems typically have the

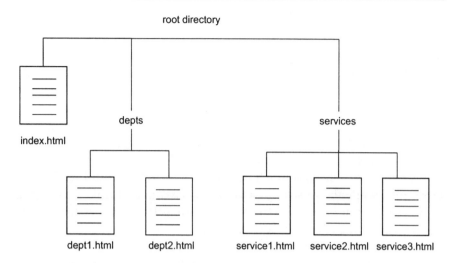

root directory

index.html

depts

services

dept1.html   dept2.html

service1.html   service2.html   service3.html

Fig. 4.2 *Diagram showing file storage structure*

extension '.html'. It is important that these extensions should be used, so that the content of files will be recognized as being in HTML.

Just as there are conventions for handling the layout of a page, there are also standard ways of handling links. In the browser, the user will see a text link as a piece of highlighted text. The text describing a link must be concise and clear. 'Click here' should never be used to indicate a link, as this says nothing about the linked content. Too many links should not be clustered together because this looks confusing. If making a link to someone else's page, indicate this by context (e.g. under a heading 'Links to other sites') or by the text of the link itself. This is to acknowledge that the content was created by someone else.

As well as from a piece of text, a single link can also be made from an image. If an image serves as a link, it will be highlighted in a user's browser. Each image should have a textual description of its link, in the form of an ALT (Alternative Text) attribute for its HTML tag (e.g. <IMG SRC="logo.gof" ALT="Image of logo">). This is for the convenience of those who cannot view the image or who have turned off image loading in their browser.

An **imagemap** is a single image containing multiple links. The image might be a composite of a number of icons, each indicating a different page on a Web site, or a plan of a building or area with links to pages describing the different sections. Imagemaps can provide useful iconic menus to guide users to information but there should always be a text-based alternative. In creating an imagemap, areas on the image must be mapped on to different links, so that when a user clicks in a particular area of an image, the correct link is activated. Specialist software and resources are available to help to create imagemaps: see the *Imagemap Help Page*.

Each link points to a file for a Web page. Links are either **absolute**, that is, quoting the full URL for the file linked to, or **relative**, which assume a site and directory path, and contain only extra path details (if any) and a file name for a page. For example, assume that we are linking from index.html in our root directory to another Web page called 'test.html' stored in a lower directory called 'work', and that our server domain is 'www.uni.ac.uk'. The absolute link would be "http://www.uni.ac.uk/work/test.html", while the relative link would be "work/test.html". Notice that the domain is totally omitted from the relative URL, as it is assumed to be the domain of the file originating the link.

When building a Web site, all links between pages on that Web site should be expressed as relative links. This is because all files stored at a particular Web site will share the site and directory path in the absolute URL for that site. Links to items on other Web sites must naturally be by absolute URL.

Finally, when adding the filename of the Web page linked by an HTML link tag, always use the extension '.html' instead of '.htm'. This works on all computer systems because those able to handle only three-character extensions will see '.html' as '.htm'. For example, on a Windows machine, a filename 'test.htm' will be found by a link looking for 'test.html'.

Links will always lead to the top of a Web page unless directed elsewhere on that page by an **anchor.** This is a piece of text in a page that has attached to it a hidden name, as a NAME tag in HTML. When this name is added to the URL of any link pointing to that page, the piece of text identified by the hidden anchor will be at the top of the browser window when the page is retrieved. Anchors are often used to create a 'table of contents' at the top of a long page, so that a user can jump to a lower section of the page without scrolling.

As with design, a good practice is to browse Web sites similar to the application area being developed, and try to ascertain their storage structures, as evidenced by pathnames in URLs. The storage structure of 'live' sites is normally the same as their offline progenitors, since this means that a copy of the site can be worked on offline and changed files etc. can be copied easily from the offline to the online site.

Chapter 5
PUBLISHING WEB SITES

The basics of publishing a Web site

Once a set of pages and associated graphics etc. have been created, publishing them is a matter of putting them onto a Web server. A server running on an intranet will limit the audience for those pages to the authorized users of that intranet. A server connected to the Internet will potentially make the audience for those pages any Internet user. Finally, there is no need to have a Web server running on a machine that is connected to any sort of network. The simplest way of 'publishing' Web pages is to run both a server and a browser on the same standalone machine. Since the 'audience' is the user of the machine running the server, this is known as a **personal Web server**.

A personal Web server is ideal for testing a Web site design. Web server software is available for most types of computer; much of this software is shareware or freeware. Once installed, running the server software will typically produce a sign (e.g. an icon showing a running program on a Windows system) showing it is ready to respond to requests for pages. If a URL of the form 'http://127.0.0.1/' is entered into a browser running on the server's machine, then the default Web page (typically 'index.html') in the root directory for Web pages will be displayed. Loading this page should cause some sort of 'server busy' message to be displayed (e.g. the Web server icon label may change to 'busy'). The difference between this mode of access to a local file and simply using the 'open local file' command in your browser is that, in the former, one is accessing a file on a working server (shown by the 'http' protocol). In the latter, the URL would start 'file://', showing that the file was merely being pulled off a local disk by the browser, without intervention from a server.

Servers typically have documentation in HTML that can be browsed when they are running. This documentation will note the location of the root directory for Web pages. On a personal Web server, copying pages for a Web site in their directory structure into this root directory will enable the Web site to be tested without fear of others seeing it. Since the pages are on a real server (albeit a limited one) it will be able to test out facilities that require server support, like form processing by CGI scripts etc.

On a Web server connected to an intranet or the Internet, if all Web pages and associated files are stored in one directory, then copying these files into the root directory on the server for Web pages will publish them (to users who know the URL). If, however, a directory structure for local files has been used, there is a need to recreate that directory structure on the Web server and make sure that the files go across into the matching directory, so that files from local directory 'test' go into directory 'test' on the server and so on.

If the server is remote (i.e. it can only be connected to via the Internet) then an **FTP (File Transfer Protocol)** package is used to copy the Web page files on to the remote server. Beware that because of file naming conventions on the server, it may be necessary to change all Web page file extensions from '.htm' to '.html' (or vice versa). The server documentation will make clear which extension is expected.

The biggest disadvantage of Web publishing in its canonical form is the problem of page and link management. Managing changes in a large number of Web pages and their associated links can become a chore. 'Search and replace' **global editor** packages are useful for changing many pages at once, for example the logo they all use.

Recently, **site management** software has become available which not only helps to create individual pages but also to manage links between the pages on a Web site. For example, these packages will notice when a locally stored page has changed and then copy it automatically on to the server, into the correct directory.

Once pages are on a Web server, but before users know of their existence, they should be **validated** (i.e. checked for certain common problems). There are a number of features that can be checked:

- Compliance with a particular HTML standard. Unvalidated HTML can crash some browsers or cause viewing irregularities. Most page creation software does not yet include validation as a feature but there are services that will validate pages without charge. Correcting the errors they throw up in pages helps build a knowledge of HTML. Other sources of 'error' can be **proprietary tags** (i.e. tags that only work properly with a particular browser). While proprietary tags may be useful, because they are not included in the HTML standard they will not work with all browsers, so try not to use them.
- Accessibility. Some Web users are visually impaired and cannot see graphics. The WAI *Accessibility Guidelines: Page Authoring,* a set of guide-

lines for making pages more accessible for people with disabilities, has been published by the Web Accessibility Initiative. *Bobby* is an online tool that analyses individual Web pages for accessibility by using a list of commonly accepted accessibility barriers.

• Links: all links should be checked to make sure they lead somewhere, otherwise they are known as **dangling links** and will annoy users. **Link checking services** will do this automatically.

Finally there are sites like *NetMechanic* and *Web Site Garage*, which collect together a range of tools for analysing pages (testing image load times, links from other sites etc.).

Web servers

A server's basic task is to send out Web pages to users on request. Servers are rated according to how many pages per second they can send out. Pushing a server beyond its limits can crash it. Shareware server software running on a PC can easily be outperformed by commercial software running on a more powerful computer. This is not to say that the most powerful server is always the best one for a task. For example, a small intranet for a handful of users could be handled easily by a server running on a PC.

Running a server is no more difficult than running a browser. Some server software is freely available, just like that for browsers: see *WebServer Compare* for a selection. Both require a machine connected to a network. However, a server needs to have a permanent link to the network, and be left running, so that browsers can access its pages at any time. Since a permanent network connection requires funding and management, individuals publish pages either freely through a server owned by their own organization or pay for disk storage space on a commercially run server.

Many institutions already have a Web server, and, through negotiation, it may be possible to put files on that server. If not, then there is always the option to use **external Web space**, that is, to put files on a server owned or run by someone else.

External Web space can either be available for a fee from a commercial supplier or it might be free. There are a number of sources of free Web space on the Internet; these are listed on the *Free Homepage Center*. Some companies who offer dial-up connection services to the Internet offer their subscribers Web space as an extra perk. There are now a large and ever-growing number of companies who will supply Web space for a fee. Many of these companies are targeting large corporate concerns as their customers; thus, buying Web space in this way will be expensive for non-corporate users. However, some of these companies are offering reasonably priced Web space for individuals. Because the World Wide Web is a global phenomenon, there is no need to seek Web space in any particular country; one should instead seek the best price. The exception is if it is expected that most users of a Web site will be from a particular country when Web space in that country would be best (as it would be near those users and thus quick to access).

The cheapest Web space is termed a **non-virtual domain** because the URL of pages include the domain name of the company supplying the Web space. If this Web space is for the user 'Bloggs', then a non-virtual domain for it might be:

http://www.webcompany.co.uk/bloggs/

A **virtual domain** looks like a separate server in its own right, but it is actually stored on the server of the company supplying the Web space. It costs more because it looks as though it is a separate server. A virtual domain for user 'Bloggs' might be:

http://www.bloggs.co.uk/

When choosing a supplier of Web space, be sure to check how much, in terms of megabytes, they offer, what server software they use, the speed of its connection to the Internet (the faster the better), what extras are available (e.g. access to CGI scripting) and, most importantly, what support facilities they offer. Some sort of conferencing system for customers to report problems ought to be provided. Beware of **resellers**, individuals who have purchased Web space from a company and who then sell parts of it on to others. However, reselling can be difficult to spot because some resellers use virtual domains to make themselves appear as a separate company! Always ask online for users' opinions when thinking of using a particular company. Finally, beware of bandwidth use charges, which can add dramatically to costs if a Web site becomes popular and sees many pages requested.

Web site promotion

Once Web pages are on a server, merely having them there is not enough to publish them properly. Potential users must be made aware that the pages exist. On an intranet this is not so difficult, as there is a captive audience, who ought to find the information on the Web pages provided to be necessary in their work. On the World Wide Web, however, the pages are competing with millions of others for attention.

To enable users to find suitable content on remote sites, two generic types of search service have evolved for World Wide Web. The first uses individuals to keep track of pages on Web sites. They do this by creating browsable subject-based **directories** of links to pages. An example of this type would be Yahoo. The second type uses **robot indexing software** (also known as crawlers or spiders) to create a searchable database of text extracted from pages at many sites. The place to go for information on how search engines work is *Search Engine Watch.*

Promoting a site on the World Wide Web involves getting a Web site covered by as many search engines as possible, especially robot search engines. A robot search engine will, once it has the URL of a Web site, periodically visit that site and add the contents to its searchable database. One can register a Web site URL with each search engine individually. However, there are a number of **registration services** that will register a site with a number of search engines at once. Those recommended are *Broadcaster* and *Submit It!* Some of these registration services are commercial. Note that registering a Web site with a search engine guarantees nothing. A robot search engine may visit the Web site only very infrequently and it may not index all the pages. However, there are free services (e.g. *PositionAgent)* that will check to see if the site has been indexed in a number of search engines. Also remember that new search engines appear over time and that a site will need to be registered with them.

It is possible to exclude some pages from robot indexing. The standard method is by *Robot Exclusion*, which involves placing a file called **'robots.txt'** in the root directory of your Web site. Commands in the 'robots.txt' file can place particular Web page files or directories off-limits to robot indexers. However, this standard has no official sanction and there are no penalties for breaching it. Never put files that should not be made public on to a server connected to the Internet.

Another problem is that individual robot search engines index pages in different ways. Because search engines operate as commercial services (they sell advertising space), their indexing strategies are normally shrouded in secrecy. Thus there is no sure way to have a site properly indexed by all search engines and ensure that it is retrieved first by searches, although there are plenty of commercial services who promise this! To ensure that the site stands a good chance of being reasonably well indexed, describe the overall content of a Web site as near to the top of the first page as possible. Be honest in the description of the Web site. *Rank This!* will report on how well pages rank with particular search engines.

Not being honest in the description, by including words that will be commonly sought but which do not match the content on the Web site, is known as **index spamming.** Another form of index spamming involves repeating the words describing a site to try to increase its ranking in the list of sites returned by searches. Index spamming is not the way to promote a Web site.

Metadata (information about content) can be added to pages. This is done by using special **meta HTML tags** to include descriptions and keywords that are used by some search engines. Meta tags can also be used to use metadata to describe a site. Currently not all search engines support metadata but this may change in the future.

To a certain extent, being covered by search engines is only one avenue of promotion. Another method is to exploit the linking with the World Wide Web. Asking related sites to make a link in exchange for a reciprocal link is a good tactic. There are **link exchange** services (some free, some commercial) that will pass users on from one site to another, by means of mutual links. Finally, one can join a **Web ring**, a group of sites on one topic, which form a chain of connecting links.

Perhaps the best promotion method is to use appropriate mailing lists and newsgroups to announce a Web site. Even better is to be recommended in these mailing lists or newsgroups by an independent source. People are far more reliable judges of content and quality than are search engines! If a Web site is regularly updated, let potential users know this by posting the contents of update pages to appropriate mailing lists and newsgroups. Set up as many feedback opportunities for a Web site as possible, to ensure that the site continues to serve its users. Use **mailto** HTML links for this (possibly one per page) and listen to user comments received. Remember, users are the reason for a Web site's existence!

Usage tracking

Attracting users is one thing. It is also wise to try to track whatever usage a Web site has. All servers keep a **usage log** showing which machine (identified by domain name) was sent which page at what time. Log analysis software (for example *Analog*) is required if the intention is to ascertain usage patterns of the server. In some situations an access log is not available in which case usage can be tracked with a **page counter**.

A usage log records only what domain requested which page at which time. A more sophisticated file known as a **cookie** can be requested from a domain and used to store the requests and actions that the user from that domain makes. Cookies are intended to be session-specific so that information about a user cannot be passed between different servers. Cookies can also be turned off by means of a browser setting to offset the privacy worries of users.

Whatever usage tracking mechanisms are employed, it is wise to recognize that users may wish for privacy. The *Platform for Privacy Preferences*

(P3P) Project is a proposed standard for privacy that will enable Web sites to express their privacy practices and users to to exercise preferences over those practices.

Finally, it is vital to build into a Web site a constant renewal and growth of information. A static Web site might initially attract users but, after a while, they will cease to come back as there will be nothing new for them. There are many (too many) Web sites that announce themselves in a blaze of enthusiasm and then slowly die because they are not updated.

For more information see Part III: 'Keeping up with World Wide Web technology' (Chapter 9).

Social and legal issues

Starting from a concept at CERN, the World Wide Web has grown into an enormous information resource on the Internet and a powerful tool for organizing local content via intranets. Because of the success of the World Wide Web as a publishing medium, commercial and governmental pressures are now shaping its destiny, just as they have for the other mass media, television and radio.

Despite its technological nature, the World Wide Web on the Internet must be seen as a medium of mass communication, taking place within a social context larger than any one Web site, shaped by an ever-changing set of principles, which are decided by the community of users as much as publishers. Since many of the users are also publishers, the range and quality of information on the Internet is vast and diverse.

Concern has been expressed over the nature of some content on the World Wide Web. There is a standard called **PICS (Platform for Internet Content Selection)**, which allows **ratings** (coded judgements on content) to be added to Web pages by their creator, but the use of ratings is voluntary and not yet widespread. There are various ratings schemes (for example RSACi) that work rather like film certification codes. As a result, access to the Internet in public places may require either that users adhere to an **acceptable use policy (AUP)** or use a software **filter**, which controls what pages may or may not be viewed in a browser. However, restricting access to information, for whatever reason, can be seen as violating freedom of speech. Whether used for controlled or uncontrolled access, a browser used in a public location should be set up in **kiosk mode** (i.e. limited to basic page retrieval and display only) in order to prevent tampering with other files or software on the browser's machine.

Unfortunately, the ease with which materials published in all media can be converted for publishing by Web sites have led to problems over copy-

35

right. Nationally and internationally, the law has yet to come to terms with copyright for material published solely by the Web.

Security is a pervasive problem on the Internet because the traffic between server and browser, whether pages or streams, is readable at every stage across the network. For most applications this is not a problem, but secure technologies are needed to support privacy, authentication and financial transactions. There are two methods, either by encoding the entire communication between a server and a browser or encoding just the content. Encoding involves using an appropriate **cryptographic standard** (for information scrambling) to ensure that information cannot be read other than by certain parties. Certain Web servers can be obtained in secure versions. Security on an intranet is normally guaranteed by eschewing external access, although a special machine/server known as a **firewall** can be used to stand between a secure intranet and the Internet. An extension of intranet is the **extranet**, a private network that functions over the Internet itself. This network is built over the public connections of the Internet using cryptographic functions to hide private traffic. It is in effect a closed network with a limited user group. It can be used to connect a group of collaborating organizations.

Applications of the World Wide Web

World Wide Web technology has also been extended to handle conferencing and real-time communications, to enable it to act like **groupware**, which facilitates people collaborating over a network. This is especially powerful over an intranet. Another development that is significant here is the idea of **push** publishing, where the server feeds a browser with changing data, for example news headlines. These data are 'pushed' from server to browser, rather than 'pulled' from server to browser on request, as is normally the case. Push publishing requires more bandwidth than the pull model (as information is being sent out without being specifically requested); this can be a significant problem.

Perhaps the most far-reaching innovation is the concept of the **network computer,** a generic type of computer that obtains all its software via the network. The idea is that all the software that users need could be written in Java and downloaded, as needed, from the World Wide Web. Therefore, users need only to store software that they regularly use on their own machine. The rest could be downloaded 'on demand', even to the extent of the operating system itself. By adding software as well, this takes to a logical conclusion the provision of all data/information via the network.

The World Wide Web has found application everywhere. Unlike other technologies that merely support current activities or operations, the

World Wide Web has proved able to transform and extend them. **E-com-merce** (business via the Internet) has grown out of businesses who started to advertise their presence via a Web site. This has broadened into selling products and services, not only to customers but between businesses themselves. The costs of commercial transactions are negligible, compared with using the traditional distribution and retail network. This has both fuelled growth and enabled the appearance of **virtual companies,** businesses that trade only via the Internet. Since marketing is a vital activity in e-commerce, search engines have become pivotal in allowing business to find customers online. Search engines are transforming themselves into **portals**, gateways into the Internet, and the services/products available through it. The Web is an ideal medium for governments to provide information about that service. The UK government, for example, is very keen on this idea and developments can be tracked through the *CCTA Government Information Service.* What is more revolutionary is that the Web can also lead to greater involvement in decision making for ordinary people, via **e-voting** systems. The future of the World Wide Web is certain; it will survive and grow. What is uncertain is how it will affect other areas of everyday life.

PART II
World Wide Web applications in UK libraries and information units

Contents

INTRODUCTION TO PART II

Part II describes the major advantages (and disadvantages) of the applications of World Wide Web technology as they affect library and information professionals in their work. See Part IV for the resources mentioned. Part III takes up, from Part I, developments in the technical side of the World Wide Web.

Chapter 6
LIBRARIES AND THE WORLD WIDE WEB

Academic libraries

In an increasingly technological society, providing Internet access is seen by many as a natural extension of the library's remit to provide information, educational and leisure services to users. The World Wide Web opens up enormous possibilities for the development and delivery of services. It offers an intuitive and increasingly familiar computing environment through which to deliver existing services and a channel for developing new ones. Services can be offered beyond the physical constraints of the library building to a wider customer base.

Academic librarians in the UK have been working in a richly networked environment for many years, with access to the Internet being freely available at point-of-use through the nationally-funded JANET (Joint Academic Network) and SuperJANET services. It is therefore not surprising that academic libraries were amongst the first wave of institutions to pioneer the development of Web pages and that today virtually all UK higher education and many further education libraries offer publicly available Web sites. National libraries and a number of national research and information centres, also linked to JANET, were similarly quick to establish a Web presence.

Although the first academic library Web pages offered little more than factual information about the library itself and links to external sites, it was not long before the Web began to be exploited as a gateway to library resources and services. Conversion of the online public access catalogue (OPAC) to Web access was often the initial starting point, which was quickly extended to making available other electronic collections (both existing and newly digitized). Academic and research libraries are still at the forefront of research and development into how best to develop and deliver electronic information resources. Information delivery is happening increasingly, although by no means exclusively, via the user's desktop

1995 to explore the shape and implementation of the electronic library of the future, researchers are investigating a whole range of topics from the digitization of text and image collections to document delivery and the on-demand publishing of books and journal articles, as and when needed by students and academics.

Public libraries

UK public libraries, hampered by lack of government support, huge demands on their budgets and lack of time for research and development, were understandably slow to follow the lead of their academic colleagues. There were isolated exceptions, such as the pioneering work undertaken on *CLIP:* Croydon Libraries Internet Project. The main theme of this project was to examine the potential of the Internet as a reference tool. Issues concerning provision of and public response to network services generally were also explored in the CLIP, and in others such as Solihull's *IT Point.*

Generally, however, public library response to the Internet was slow to get off the ground. According to the only comprehensive national survey of Internet connectivity in UK public libraries so far (the *Library and Information Commission public library Internet survey*), although 53% of public library authorities had some sort of Internet connection by 1995, most were restricted to use by staff only, generally at one or two workstations to support reference services. Nationally, there were only 39 public access workstations available. In 1994, *Project EARL* (Electronic Access to Resources in and through Libraries) was initiated as a coalition of interested parties within the library and information community, to coordinate the development of electronic networks for information and to facilitate the exchange of information and experience. EARL's approach has been pragmatic, offering help and advice to member authorities.

Although the proportion of UK public branch libraries with Internet access is still pitifully small, in partnership with EARL, many public library authorities have now constructed Web sites for the public to access from computers in major branches or, for those who can, from home, work and other external locations. As yet, the main thrust has been on the provision of information about the library and its services, rather than on service delivery. At the time of writing, only a handful of UK public library authorities have provided access to their catalogues via the Internet, for example, although quite a number maintain searchable databases of local and community information. In an influential report that is beginning to stimulate a response from Government, entitled *New Library: the People's Network*, the Library and Information Commission has examined how public libraries can and should exploit information and networking technologies.

Special libraries and information units

Only a small proportion of UK private sector libraries offer a public access Web site, although there are public relations benefits to be gained by doing so. For example, a wealth of corporate data collected by their library is available on the *Shell International* Web site, including company news and press releases, corporate literature, public briefing papers on industry related subjects, selected technical papers and more. More typically, the UK corporate librarian is involved in the design, development and maintenance of Web pages for internal consumption on the corporate intranet or extranet rather than providing a public service.

The UK section of the *BUBL Information Service* (originally Bulletin Board for Libraries) offers a good directory of Web sites from UK public sector libraries and library organizations, including national, public and academic libraries. Public library sites are listed on *UK Public Libraries on the Web*, while Project EARL lists member libraries. *NISS* (National Information Services and Systems) offers key directories of UK educational and research libraries and OPACs. NISS and BUBL are also good starting points for tracing library Web sites world-wide and library related resources and issues. *UKOLN*, the UK Office for Library and Information Networking, provides links to research on library networking and digitization. Although with an American public library bias, Jerry Kuntz's *Library Land* is another starting point for library resources.

Many Web projects, not just in libraries, have started small and grown well beyond initial expectations until resources have had to be diverted to sustain developments. Gone are the days when the Web site of an organization is managed and maintained by enthusiasts as a side-line activity. Many Web initiatives that began in the library have become the responsibility of the parent organization, with dedicated staff and a committee structure, editorial board or steering group to advise on the design, content and makeup of the Web site and on the management of the project. The library itself will often make a strong contribution to this development team and, depending on local policy, will have more or less autonomy for the look, feel and content of its own pages on the organizational site. Such is the model for many CWIS (Campus Wide Information Systems) from universities and colleges. In only relatively few public sector organizations has the library retained overall responsibility for the institutional Web site, even then it is often in partnership with other departments and sections.

Chapter 7
WORLD WIDE WEB APPLICATIONS IN LIBRARIES

Overview

Before embarking on a Web development project, many fundamental questions need to be addressed from the outset. How is the site going to be financed, managed and resourced, and can/should it be done within the constraints of existing budgets and staffing levels? Will more, or more powerful, computers and networking facilities be needed? How can it be justified to the organization? Will staff roles and responsibilities change and, if so, how will this be managed? What is the purpose of the Web site and what should it be designed to achieve? Who will use it and how can it best serve their requirements? How will users' needs be assessed and then monitored? Should certain client groups be prioritized, and what about providing pages for library staff? How can staff and users be trained or guided to use the site to good advantage? What impact will it have on the provision of existing collections and services? Pages that are designed to be used predominantly by members of an institution, and whose interests are reasonably well-known, will need a very different design philosophy to pages aimed at a heterogeneous group of 'virtual' users who share little except a common, but possibly only a passing, interest in a site.

Answers to these and many other questions will shape fundamentally the design and contents of a site. Nevertheless there are lessons to be learnt and ideas to be gained from libraries that have already started on the journey. The following sections indicate some of the features that libraries of all types, but predominantly academic and public libraries, are incorporating into their public access Web pages. Hopefully, they will provide ideas, inspiration and advice for others about to embark on a similar venture. Our focus is on content rather than design or policy. Public access policy issues have been identified in a preliminary report from the Project EARL *Policy Issues/Public Access Strategies Task Group*.

Public relations, promotion and sales

Web pages offer an unprecedented new opportunity for libraries to promote their image and services. Unfortunately, there are many instances where this opportunity has not been seized and where pages are uninspired in both design and content. In contrast, well designed pages can present an image of the library that is professional, pleasant and responsive to user needs. They can draw attention to services that clients might otherwise overlook. Sheila and Robert Harden, on the UK Public Libraries part of their Web page, suggest that well-designed pages should offer:

- interactive features for example, opportunities for users to provide feedback, participate in online events or contribute to certain pages;
- real information that is not available elsewhere on the Internet, such as local information;
- site development, in other words, a site that is not static but clearly evolves to reflect current information and initiatives;
- network guidance to help the library's particular clientele to locate and use other, appropriate Internet resources.

The home page is the key not only to the range of information at the site but also the image to be projected; it is worth paying some attention to its content and design. Too many library home pages look very textual, with little more than a logo or picture by way of graphical content. The *North Lincolnshire Libraries'* site takes a conventional but well-designed approach, while *City of Leeds: Library and Information Services, Essex Libraries, Nottinghamshire County Council Library Services* and *Shell International* offer more graphical styles.

There are no hard-and-fast rules about what information and links should go on the home page, but for most libraries the essentials are contact details (name, address, telephone, opening hours), a friendly welcome and links to services, supplemented by some 'quick facts' on core services. A few facts and figures on the collection size and the number of loans, acquisitions and enquiries can portray an image of a dynamic organization, handling and managing large quantities of information and materials on behalf of its customers. Any unusual services can be prominently displayed to challenge the stereotypical, dull image of libraries generally, and to draw attention to the range and diversity of library provision. (In the research for this chapter, special services as diverse as computer equipment hire and T-shirt printing were encountered!)

Some libraries offer a newsletter or announcements on their Web pages to promote special events, services or exhibitions. Others promote the use of their collections, for example, via new books lists, reviews or profiling of selected items such as 'the millionth volume'. Obviously these pages must be updated frequently, unlike the more static information mentioned in the last paragraph.

Library research activities and publications may be highlighted and, although technically more advanced, interactive ordering of publications or other sale items can be introduced, with descriptive text and images of dust jackets or covers to add visual impact.

Service and contact information

The fundamental role and purpose of the library will define what information it can and should provide about itself on public access pages. Typical examples might include:

- details of core and special services;
- descriptions or guides to the various collections and facilities;
- FAQs about the library including the obvious – how to join, borrow and renew materials;
- service statistics (with or without appropriate interpretation);
- a staff directory, organized by department, responsibilities etc.;
- location maps (including local transport and mobile library routes, and nearby car parking);
- A–Z listings of sites within a multisite organization or a cooperative, linked to separate pages giving branch details, address/contact information and opening times;
- scanned images of floor plans through to multimedia library tours offering, for example, spoken messages from staff, organizational structure, mission statement, regulations and policy documents.

To add a personal touch, staff contact names can be added to the description of each service as well as listed in directory-style from a list of services on or just below the home page, although public libraries in particular are cautious about naming individual members of staff.

User queries, participation and feedback

Libraries are offering interactivity on their Web pages in three main areas:

- online enquiries and requests;
- user-driven services;
- general feedback and suggestions.

The opportunities to offer online enquiries and requests ranges from 'ask a librarian' type reference questions, through submission of literature, online search and interlibrary loan requests and purchase recommendations, to special services such as room and equipment booking. Perhaps the most prominent examples of reference enquiry forms is the Internet Public Library's *IPL Ask a Question Form* and EARL's *Ask a Librarian.*

A community notice board is the foremost example of a user-driven service, with library customers supplying details of local events, lost and found items and the like. Some public libraries have even experimented with user-supplied book or Internet site reviews. User-supplied reviews are not, however, widespread on UK library sites, they are inevitably vulnerable to facetious or misleading contributions or worse. It is always wise to vet customers' contributions before loading them on a server and to put a disclaimer on the relevant Web pages to alert users to the vetting procedure. It is also advisable to withdraw information either routinely after a fixed interval or by regular weeding.

Because the Web is so new and unbounded it can be hard to determine just how well a site is supporting clients' interests and information needs. It is therefore worth soliciting feedback, either by a suggestion box linked to particular services or pages, or by a general 'tell us how we are doing' section on the Web site. Invite suggestions for new resources and links. User feedback can even be turned to wider strategic advantage, for example an academic library in the USA used its Web site to ask users to send messages of support for a new library building campaign.

Whenever feedback is invited, contributors should obviously be asked to submit their name and contact details, not only to facilitate a response to them but to encourage responsible commentary. Respond quickly to all suggestions received, even if it is only to send a routine acknowledgement.

The simplest approach to implementing user feedback on your Web site, but the most difficult to deal with systematically at the receiving end, is simply to invite responses via e-mail. This will be necessary if the user's browser does not support forms. The e-mail facility in the user's browser can be activated automatically, as at the 'Contact us' section at the Internet Public Library site. Otherwise, it is worthwhile giving guidelines on what information the user should always include with the e-mail message.

In most situations it is far more convenient to provide a standard form, albeit with a section for unstructured comment, to ensure some consistency in the details submitted. The low-tech solution is a form that the user can print and post or fax back, or complete and return via e-mail. CGI scripted forms are the standard solution. Many American examples of CGI scripted Web forms used by libraries can be found at *The Library Web*

Manager's Reference Center.

One of the biggest problems from the library end of facilitating user participation via a public access Web site is authentication of users' requesting services, such as interlibrary loan, for example. Providing access to a circulation database to cross-check user details is technically complex and would certainly require programming support. A simpler solution, although one that requires a certain duplication of effort, is to maintain a separate list of registered users and obtain a PERL script to match the user-supplied details with the list. A polite but firm standard response could be sent automatically to unauthorized users. The circumstances in some libraries may make it possible to restrict access to the forms facility to machines in specified domains so that, for example, requests could be submitted only from terminals in the library or the institution. The simplest solution of all, and still probably the most common, is to do a manual check on registration details, as would normally be the case for requests submitted on paper.

Training and instruction

The range of training activities offered from library Web pages ranges from traditional bibliographic and library instruction, through tutorials on using particular databases and systems, to guidance on using and searching the Internet generally or the library Web pages in particular. Some academic librarians are working in partnership with lecturers to provide course-specific information retrieval skills across a range of information resources, or providing links from the library pages to computer-based training materials across a range of subject areas.

Development of training programmes should not be embarked upon lightly. It is expensive in terms of time and resources and, if product-related, can be particularly frustrating when particular information products or tools are changed and upgraded. Happily, there is a wealth of training material on the Web and the reader is referred to the excellent *Netskills* training service which, although developed within the higher education fraternity, leads to training materials and opportuities that are relevant to both the public and private sectors.

Library databases

Most major library system suppliers now offer a gateway product to enable the library catalogue(s) to be searched directly from a Web browser. Many (though by no means all) UK academic libraries have installed such software, the main alternative being a simple telnet link to the local library automation system. Increasingly, national research centres, archives, information services and professional associations also offer OPAC searching via the Web. The BUBL Information Service maintains a fairly up-to-date list of network-accessible UK OPACs. As yet, relatively few UK public libraries offer OPAC searching via the Internet, but some examples can be found on the *UK Public Libraries on the Web* service. *SALSER* (Scottish Academic Library Serials), a searchable catalogue of serials from a consortium of Scottish academic and research libraries, was one of the first Internet-accessible union catalogues to be offered in the UK.

A Web front-end for OPAC searching offers many improvements over other alternatives. It is familiar and intuitive to many users and hypertext navigation can facilitate searching if useful links are provided, for example, links between separate collections or to works by the same author, publisher or on the same subject as a found item. Hypertext can also facilitate jumps to other functions provided by the library automation system, such as the loan status of an item, patron-activated reservations or personal borrowing information. Context-sensitive help and user training can be linked from appropriate points on each screen. Forms can be provided to input the search request. Other advantages of a Web OPAC include the option to download search results via e-mail and FTP, and the facility to display special characters from non-Roman scripts more easily than with many other software alternatives.

As might be imagined, however, integrating an existing library automation system with the library's Web interface involves complex functionality and needs to be carried out in consultation with the library's system suppliers. To minimize technical problems, some institutions make the Web version of the OPAC available on dedicated terminals within the library itself.

In addition to the OPAC to search the main catalogue or special collections, other examples of locally compiled data sets that libraries are presenting via the Web include: calendars of events, courses and exhibitions, either within the library itself, the parent institution or the region; booklists ('top titles', recommendations and reviews, or recent acquisitions) and guides to the literature; and FAQs dealing with recurring reference and information enquiries. Unlike the OPAC, of course, these can be presented using standard Web technology, and do not require a special-purpose search engine. When designing menu structures to access this type of information, an attempt should be made to try to think of alternative arrangements that might be useful. Events, for example, are often listed by type but an alternative might be to provide a 'what's on' calendar: click on a date and the events for that day are displayed.

A number of UK public library authorities (at the time of writing these include Cambridge, Hertfordshire, Islington, Kingston, Manchester City and Norfolk, and also Croydon Online, Liverpool, Somerset, Surrey, Barnsley and Leeds) have introduced searchable community information databases. These may be completely new data collections, planned in collaboration with other departments or agencies, or conversions of existing viewdata or videotext services. Typically, these might include council and community information such as local clubs, societies, community and voluntary organizations, events and exhibitions calendars, lists of local councillors and officers etc. Some public library authorities have built strong links with public and private sector organizations in their area to cover a broader spectrum of local information, also including tourism, leisure, health, job vacancies and more.

In the academic sector, much research and development is under way under the auspices of the *ELib programme* (Chapter 6) and elsewhere to further the realization of the digital library. Research ranges over a spectrum of areas including electronic document delivery, on-demand publishing and digitization. This is fuelling the number of Web-accessible full-text, as well as bibliographic and image, collections available to library users, although access is normally restricted to members of institutions participating in particular projects. Less ambitiously, reading lists by course name or lecturer name and other teaching and learning resources, are now expected, linked directly from the library home page, from departmental pages on the institutional Web site and/or from a special section of the OPAC.

Digitization of special collections such as incunabula, rare photographs, maps, sound archives and other materials, can help to solve the dual problems of preservation of and access to rare or fragile materials. The *American Memory* project from the Library of Congress and the British Library's *Initiatives for Access* project have done much pioneering work. The *University of Houston Libraries' Special Collections on the Web* is a good starting point to trace projects.

One can hardly begin to contemplate the wealth of materials in libraries, archives and local history collections that could usefully be made available electronically. Although the task seems overwhelming, progress is beginning in the UK. For example, EARL Development, part of Project EARL, has a number of task groups charged with making available, via the Web library, collections in specialist areas such as music and poetry.

Leased databases

Libraries and information centres were once the major, if not the only, customers of commercial electronic information providers. With the advent of the Web, a burgeoning number of commercial providers have set up services aimed at other market sectors, particularly home and business endusers. Established vendors have begun to respond to this challenge by developing Web interfaces for their own services. Web versions of some of the major online subscription services (*BIDS*), *OCLC FirstSearch*, *MED-LINE, EBSCO, DIALOG Web, Ovid*) are now established and can be linked directly from the library pages. Once connected, users need a password to log in. If the service is subscription rather than connect time based it is feasible to offer connections from public access terminals in the library. For example, DIALOG charges are now processor, not connect time, based.

User authentication is essential wherever a link is provided to a leased or licensed service. Some library systems suppliers offer a Z39.50 option from the OPAC for remote database searching, in other words, a gateway between HTTP and Z39.50 databases. The gateway needs to offer access control and authentication, and would normally restrict access for external users (i.e. those connecting from outside the organization) to the OPAC and other local databases only.

There are many good examples amongst academic libraries, for example Miami University Libraries Information Network (*MIAMILINK*), provides information about and links to a large number of electronic databases, the majority of which are available as Web versions, although a few are still Telnet or Gopher accessible only. Databases are listed alphabetically by name with a brief description of each one, which is far more helpful than listing under service provider (*BIDS, OCLC FirstSearch* etc.). With the former arrangement, users need to be told which service password to enter, but adequate security on automatic password entry can be offered if the service is blocked to terminals outside the institution.

Links to other Internet resources

Maintaining links is a time consuming business and resources need to be committed to do it properly. Moreover, links can be seen as an implicit validation of a remote site, even if a disclaimer is provided to the contrary. Some organizations, particularly in the private sector, do not, therefore, as a matter of policy, provide links from their Web pages to external resources.

Despite these reservations, the World Wide Web offers librarians an unprecedented opportunity to enhance their role as information providers by opening up a gateway to information that has never before been easily available to their users. Depending on local policy, links to selected resources may be made from the library's own pages or from those of the parent institution, or from both. Whatever the position, library staff are well qualified to select and evaluate information resources, and are failing in their role if they are not pivotal in the selection and maintenance of any links on their institutional Web site.

Links on library Web sites range from apparently *ad hoc* lists of search engines, with little or no information other than the name of the engine and its URL, through to careful selections, chosen with the library's particular clientele in mind and supported by guidance to help the user understand when and how to use the remote service. *South Ayrshire Council: Libraries & Information Services*, for example, offer a good selection of links to UK online magazines and newspapers, resources for children, and links to local interest topics such as golf.

Assuming an understanding of user needs, how does one go about compiling a set of suitable links to other Internet resources and library catalogues? Certain links may be prescribed by corporate policy, such as those to and from the parent organization's home page or links to collaborating organizations or departments.

User and subject-based collections of national and international links compiled with quality in mind by the library and information community are enormously useful, and many can be traced via *BUBL Link*. Some that are worthy of particular mention because of their UK provenance include, for the public library community:

* *EARLWeb* – a compilation of Internet sites targeted at public library users;

and for researchers, lecturers and professional practice:

* *ADAM* – art, design, architecture and the media;
* *Biz/ed* – a business and economics gateway targeted at students, teachers and lecturers;
* *Business information sources on the Internet;*
* *ChemDex* – chemistry;
* *EEVL* – engineering;
* *ELDIS* – electronic development and environment;
* *History;*
* *HUMBUL* – humanities;
* *OMNI* – biomedicine;
* *PICK* – library and information science;
* *RUDI* – urban design;
* *SOSIG* – social sciences.

Local or regional information for an individual area is worth considering for libraries of all types. It is surprising how few university CWIS have seized the opportunity to provide a gateway to any local services for staff and students. In local authorities, responsibility for providing local and community information links may rest with the authority itself with the library service as a participating partner, or be devolved to the library and information service; but, as might be expected, this is an area of rapid growth and development of Web pages with some excellent examples to be found.

Links that might be considered include:

- **community information**: local authority pages; citizen's advice bureau; job centres; community organizations.
- **education**: educational establishments offering courses at all levels; local authority education pages.
- **business**: major local companies; chambers of commerce; business links; trading standards; economic development initiatives; tourism and travel agencies, including local transport operators and taxi firms; small businesses or professional practices in selected lines of business.
- **recreation and leisure**: sporting and cultural venues; leisure centres, theatres and cinemas; local clubs and societies.

A link to the local newspaper's site (if there is one) is often a good bet. As yet the number of UK regional newspapers offering Web sites is modest, but they are set to follow the trend set by the nationals, several of which offer excellent sites. Many of the regional newspaper sites that do exist offer a rich mine of local information such as 'what's on', 'things to do' and job vacancies, as well as local news and business stories organized by subject.

Moving further afield, it becomes more difficult to identify and evaluate suitable resources, but, happily, many services exist that make life easier for the rest of us. Of particular relevance to academic and public libraries respectively, both *BUBL* and *Project EARL* (Chapter 6) maintain gateways to Internet search engines, reference works, electronic journals and texts and much more.

If it is decided to incorporate links to gateway services like these, always consider:

- the source, reliability and completeness of information on the site;
- its relevance (in terms of both content and organization) to users;
- the commitment of the site to updating its resources and maintaining its links;

- the authority of the site, its funding basis and likely stability;
- the reliability and ease of connection to the site (servers in your own country are usually a better bet);
- whether the site requires special software to be browsable on your machines.

Once suitable sites have been identified, remember that it is a courtesy to seek the approval of their owners before installing a link from one's own site.

Filtering

However carefully links are chosen for the library pages, the nature of the World Wide Web defies any collection policy in the established sense. Users will inevitably find their way to material that is inaccurate, out of date or untrustworthy and possibly, whether by accident or design, to material that is objectionable, obscene or illegal. Until now, librarians have made a professional decision about what materials to put in libraries. The Internet raises both the serious risk of the library being seen as a supplier of illegal subject matter and the knotty problem of addressing the criteria that define what is and what is not acceptable to be viewed in a public place or through a professional information service. As well as the legal, moral and ethical questions that arise, many librarians are concerned that the reputation of the library will be damaged if it is seen to take a *laissez faire* attitude.

A number of measures should be considered. One is to alert users to the issue and to provide some tips on how to assess the veracity of a site. Another is to provide a very carefully targeted set of resources with the aim of reducing people's reliance on search engines that can easily produce links to unreliable material. As far as illegal or unacceptable material is concerned, an increasingly common approach is to publish an acceptable use policy. As yet there is no agreement on what such a policy should cover.

More controversially, the use of filtering software can be used to block information from specific sites or newsgroups, or material containing specified keywords. The former approach is more common on newer filters because of the poor reliability of software based on keyword filters, which can block legitimate sites as well as dubious ones. Individual libraries may wish to amend the list of banned sites associated with a particular filter but this is not always possible. The *Internet Filter Assessment Project* was a major initiative by some 40 American librarians to assess the major filters on the market in 1997.

Although many UK libraries are still formulating a policy on filtering, the issue is a contentious one in the USA. There the debate is polarized, represented at the two extremes by the positions of the American Civil Liberties Union and the American Library Association (ALA) versus pressure groups such as Filtering Facts and Family Friendly Libraries. The ALA's *Resolution on the use of filtering software in libraries* expresses the firm opinion that the use of such software violates principles of free speech and its own Bill of Rights. *Filtering Facts* was set up by a professional librarian to challenge the ALA's position. It puts the pro-filtering arguments and reports on cases of child and adult access to pornography, as well as listing some recommended filters. 'Family Friendly Libraries' is the site of an organization which lobbies public libraries to consider local values in deveopling their collections.

Z39.50 and the World Wide Web

Z39.50 was orginally proposed in 1984 as a standard way of searching bibliographic databases. It is integrated into several library management systems available from larger suppliers. The problem with Web search engines and Web enabled OPACs is that they all differ according to the provider, either in their user interface or the search features they offer. Z39.50 offers the prospect of a standard interface for searching *ad hoc* groupings of databases such as OPACs, CD-ROMs, local non-bibliographic databases and remote online services, as well as extended facilities such as interlibrary loans.

There are a variety of ways that Z39.50 can be configured for the World Wide Web, both at the server and the client end, or via a WWW-Z39.50 gateway. Outside the library and information community, the implementation of Z39.50 at the server end has been a low priority because of the lack of 'visibility' it brings to individual service providers. Although some within the library and information service community would argue that a World Wide Web interface is sufficiently familiar and intuitive not to warrant the additional investment in Z39.50, there is a strong lobby in its favour.

An overview of Z39.50 and its implications for libraries can be found on the *Z39.50 Maintenance Agency* site at the Library of Congress. For information on UK implementations see the *Directory of Z39.50 targets in the UK.*

Part III
Developments in World Wide Web technology

|||

Contents

INTRODUCTION TO PART III

The objective of this chapter is to introduce some elements of Web technology in more detail, particularly those requiring some technical knowledge. However, no knowledge of the World Wide Web, apart from that given in Part I, is assumed. Cited resources are to be found in Part IV.

Chapter 8
FUNDAMENTAL WEB TECHNOLOGY

HTTP and HTML

As HTTP has developed, requests for extensions and new features have grown. As a result, **HyperText Transfer Protocol – next generation (HTTP-NG)** is an attempt to design and prototype a new generation HTTP using current best practice in protocol design. HTML 4.0 provides a number of new features, together with some already covered, such as CSS:

- *Unicode,* an international language encoding standard, has been incorporated with HTML 4.0 and will eventually replace ASCII. The World Wide Web still has a bias towards English and other Roman scripts. The introduction of Unicode is intended to help to overcome this bias.
- The *Document Object Model (DOM)* provides ways for scripts to manipulate HTML defined independently of particular programming languages or computer platforms. It forms the basis for dynamic effects in Web pages, but can also be used by other software for manipulating HTML directly. For example, a graphics program might change simultaneously a logo that is an object in a number of Web pages,.
- **Dynamic HTML** is a term used to describe HTML pages with content that changes as a result of user interaction. It is a way of standardizing the user interactivity now carried out by diverse client-side programming languages such as Javascript etc. CSS is one of three components in dynamic HTML; the other two are HTML itself and JavaScript (which is being standardized under the name **EcmaScript**). The three components are 'glued' together with DOM, the component object model. Dynamic HTML is still in its infancy and current implementations are experimental, although the current generation of browsers is slowly embracing it.

HTML has proceeded through a number of versions because the problem is that it consists of a fixed set of tags. Introducing new tags involves obtaining a consensus of the World Wide Web community. **XML (Extensible Markup Language)** is a potential replacement for HTML because it is not a single markup language but rather a metalanguage for designing markup languages. Unlike a regular markup language (e.g. HTML), which defines a way to describe information in a certain class of documents, XML allows the definition of customized markup languages for many classes of document. XML is simpler to use for this purpose than SGML.

Resource description

Just as XML is a replacement for HTML, problems with URLs (essentially the lack of volatility of the files to which they point) and the lack of metadata incorporated in Web pages have been addressed. URLs are essentially a type of **URI (Uniform Resource Identifier)**, the set of addresses for network resources and a higher level standard for URLs. Another type of URI is a **URN (Uniform Resource Name)**, which is distinguished from a URL in that it is a guarantee (usually by a certain institution) that the address it points to will persist indefinitely. So far, the only working example is the **PURL (Persistent Uniform Resource Locator)**. Functionally, a PURL is a URL. However, instead of pointing directly to the location of an Internet resource, a PURL points to an intermediate resolution service. The PURL resolution service associates the PURL with the actual URL and returns that URL to the client.

Related to URIs and URNs is the **URC (Uniform Resource Citation, or Uniform Resource Characteristics)**. An URC is a set of attribute/value pairs describing a resource. Examples of attributes might be authorship, publisher, datatype, date, copyright status etc. Each of these attributes would be given a value with an appropriate descriptive string, for example K. Robinson, Ecotage International, etc. This is essentially metadata about the resource described.

The most commonly used standard for metadata is the **Dublin Core**, which is a 15-element metadata element set intended to facilitate the discovery of electronic resources. Originally conceived for author-generated description of Web resources, it has also attracted the attention of formal resource description communities such as museums and libraries. The Dublin Core is intended to be usable by non-cataloguers as well as by those with cataloguing experience. Its 15 elements are intended to be useable across a wide variety of disciplines, although there is flexibility to add elements to the basic set if warranted.

The **Resource Description Framework (RDF)** is a specification currently under development, which is designed as general support for metadata standards such as the Dublin Core. RDF will allow different metadata standards to be defined but will provide a uniform and interoperable means to exchange metadata between different standards. Furthermore, RDF will provide a means for publishing both a human-readable and a machine-understandable definition of the metadata itself. RDF will use XML as the transfer syntax in order to use standard tools being built for XML.

Chapter 9
ASSOCIATED WEB TECHNOLOGY

CGI and server-side scripting

PERL is available as freeware (as well as commercially) and has many tutorials available. For those not wishing to delve into PERL, there are libraries of ready made CGI scripts available for download. It is not obligatory to use PERL; just about any computer language that can create programs can be used.

As with CGI scripting, a reasonable level of technical knowledge is required to use **server-side scripting**, which is different from CGI in that the scripting functionality is built into the server itself, rather than being supplied by an external piece of software. It is wrong always to think that pages stored on a server are **static**, that is, unchanging once they are stored on the server. Pages that can be customized by a server according to particular requests are known as **dynamic** pages. There are two advantages of using dynamic pages, quite apart from their ability to be tailored to users' requests.

First, pages are typically created from common elements. Dynamic pages allow this to be done efficiently. One method of creating dynamic Web pages is the **server-side include** mechanism. Some servers can be configured to recognize pages ending in '.shtml' instead of '.html' as pages that it should scan for server-side include commands that are referencing other files. These files are added to the content of the '.shtml' Web page, to form the complete page. The idea is that these component files are generic across Web pages (e.g. containing a logo). It is then only necessary to change one of these component files, when all the Web pages that include that file will also be changed. Along similar lines are **Active Server Pages**, a Microsoft product for their Web servers.

Second, dynamic pages can be created from information held in other systems. For example, a source of dynamic Web pages can be a database linked to a server. This can be an extremely efficient way of publishing pages because the data from the database forms their content, which is output from the database with appropriate tags, thus forming HTML pages for the server to output. Content can be then created according to user-supplied information (e.g. if a user asks to see product information, this can be pulled from a product database and formatted as a Web page).

Client-side programming

Client-side programming has already been introduced in Part I, as a way of allowing a user's browser to run an application downloaded as part of a Web page. While client-side programming languages are not part of fundamental Web technology, they certainly now play a large role in how the Web functions. Using them does not need a sound knowledge of programming, but this would certainly be of considerable help even when using the most basic scripts/routines/applets. You have been warned!

There are libraries of applets for Java, and routines for other languages (especially Javascript and ActiveX) available for download, together with tutorials and programming tools for those who want to develop their own interactive Web page applications

Keeping up with World Wide Web technology

This book can cover only a limited range of Web technologies. There are a number of sites that try to offer the Webmaster guidance in all areas, from basic HTML through to multimedia, CGI/client/server-side programming and design techniques. Sites such as *BUILDER.COM, Webmonkey, The HTML Writers Guild* and the *Web Developer's Virtual Library,* cover an enormous amount of ground and can serve as a sole source of information, much like a voluminous, but always updated, reference book.

PART IV
World Wide Web resource guide

IV

Contents

INTRODUCTION TO PART IV

How to read the resource guide

The resource guide is organized into broad sections that follow the same sequence as the main text. Within each section, resources are arranged in the order in which they are cited in the text, together with additional uncited resources. To locate useful resources, browse the entries in the appropriate section/s.

If the resource sought has a recognized name, it will be locatable via the Index to the book.

Each resource has been described according to a standard template:

- **Name:** full name of the resource, usually the title of the opening Web page;
- **Provider:** organizational and/or personal name of the provider;
- **Description:** factual description of the resource;
- **URL(s):** one or more URLS, giving a UK or European location if available.

Resources were last checked between July and August, 1998. Details may have changed since then.

Resources linked to Part I

Chapter 1
THE CONCEPT OF THE WORLD WIDE WEB

NAME Tim Berners-Lee

PROVIDER Tim Berners-Lee

DESCRIPTION Biographical information about the founder of the World Wide Web. It lists his recent articles about developments of the WWW and gives contact information.

URL(S) http://www.w3.org/People/Berners-Lee/

NAME Information Management: A Proposal

PROVIDER W3 Consortium (W3C)

DESCRIPTION The original proposal, dated March 1989, uncorrected and unchanged from the Word for Mac original, which set out the concept of the World Wide Web. Well worth reading just to see how the concept appeared in its original context, as a research proposal at CERN.

URL(S) http://www.w3.org/History/1989/proposal.html

Hypertext

NAME As We May Think

PROVIDER Denys Duchier (duchier@cs.sfu.ca)

DESCRIPTION A reproduction, with permission, of the original article by Vannevar Bush from the July 1945 issue of *The Atlantic Monthly*. Text and compressed versions are available for download. Includes a link to the Bush Symposium, 12–13October 1995, MIT (Massachusetts Institute of Technology), a celebration of Vannevar Bush's 1945 vision.

URL(S) http://www.isg.sfu.ca/~duchier/misc/vbush/

NAME **[alt.hypertext] Frequently Asked Questions (FAQ list)**
PROVIDER Jamie Blustein (jamie@csd.uwo.ca)
DESCRIPTION Frequently-asked questions (FAQ) document posted fortnightly to the alt.hypertext newsgroup. A good starting point of information on hypertext and hypermedia.

> **URL(s)** http://www.lib.ox.ac.uk/internet/news/faq/archive/
> hypertext-faq.html
> http://www.csd.uwo.ca/~jamie/hypertext-faq.html

The History of the World Wide Web

NAME **History and Development of the Internet and WWW**
PROVIDER Gregory R. Gromov (gromov@internetvalley.com)
DESCRIPTION A rather over-designed but fascinating scrap book of quotes and images which gives an entertaining account of the growth of the Internet and the World Wide Web. Includes a quiz.

> **URL(s)** http://www.internetvalley.com/intval.html

NAME **IETF Home Page**
PROVIDER Internet Engineering Task Force (IETF)
DESCRIPTION The IETF is a large open international community of individuals concerned with the evolution of Internet architecture. Its work is done by a myriad of working groups, which are organized by topic into several areas. Much of the work is handled via mailing lists.

> **URL(s)** http://www.ietf.org/

NAME **World Wide Web FAQ**
PROVIDER Thomas Boutell (boutell@boutell.com)
DESCRIPTION FAQ document last dated 1996 covering all things related to the World Wide Web. Available in text and compressed forms for download. Being replaced by 'open' FAQs at time of writing.

> URL(s) http://info.ox.ac.uk/help/wwwfaq/
> http://www.boutell.com/faq/oldfaq/index.html

NAME **W3C – The World Wide Web Consortium**
PROVIDER W3C
DESCRIPTION Since 1994, the World Wide Web Consortium has been the driving force behind standards for the Web. It is the site to check for technical information and announcements of new developments.

> **URL(s)** http://www.w3.org/

Intranets

NAME **Complete Intranet Resource**
PROVIDER Intrack.com
DESCRIPTION Excellent collection of FAQs, articles, resources, a discussion board etc. The site is keyword searchable.
> **URL(s)** http://www.intrack.com/intranet/

NAME **Inside the Intranet**
PROVIDER CMP Net Inc.
DESCRIPTION Contains some good articles but is very strong in terms of case studies. Three example, living, intranet sites are presented, from J. P. Morgan, Deere & Co. and Westinghouse.
> **URL(s)** http://pubs.cmpnet.com/internetwk/intranet/
> intranet.html

NAME **Intranets – Welcome from the Mining Co.**
PROVIDER General Internet Inc.
DESCRIPTION Informative site, with information on related topics such as extranet and knowledge management.
> **URL(s)** http://intranets.miningco.com/

Chapter 2
FUNDAMENTAL TECHNOLOGY OF THE WORLD WIDE WEB

NAME **BrowserWatch Home Page**
PROVIDER Internet.com
DESCRIPTION Contains information and news about browsers, browser plug-ins and usage statistics.
> **URL(s)** http://browserwatch.internet.com/

NAME **Internet Servers**
PROVIDER Mecklermedia Corporation
DESCRIPTION A comprehensive guide to Internet servers, with news, server popularity listings and ratings, and extensive reviews of Web servers (among others).
> **URL(s)** http://serverwatch.internet.com/

Hypertext Transfer Protocol (HTTP)

NAME **HyperText Transfer Protocol – HTTP/1.1**
PROVIDER W3C
DESCRIPTION Specification for the HTTP/1.1 protocol
> **URL(s)** http://www.w3.org/Protocols/rfc2068/rfc2068

HyperText Markup Language (HTML)

NAME **HTML 4.0 Specification**
PROVIDER W3C
DESCRIPTION Specification for the latest version of HTML (4.0 at the time of writing).
> **URL(s)** http://www.w3.org/TR/REC-html40/

Uniform Resource Locators (URLs)

NAME   Uniform Resource Locators
PROVIDER   W3C
DESCRIPTION   URL specification
URL(s)   http://www.w3.org/Addressing/URL/Overview.
html

Chapter 3
CREATING WEB PAGES

Page creation tools

NAME   **Yahoo! UK & Ireland – HTML Editors**
PROVIDER   Yahoo! Inc.
DESCRIPTION   Listing of HTML editors by platform and by company.
URL(s)   http://www.yahoo.co.uk/Computers_and_
Internet/Software/Internet/World_Wide_Web/
HTML_Editors/

NAME   **Yahoo! UK & Ireland – HTML Convertors**
PROVIDER   Yahoo! Inc.
DESCRIPTION   A good listing of commercial and freeware convertors.
URL(s)   http://www.yahoo.co.uk/Computers_and_
Internet/Software/Internet/World_Wide_Web/
HTML_Converters/

Page layout and structure

NAME   **CSS Gallery**
PROVIDER   Microsoft Corporation
DESCRIPTION   Microsoft's view of CSS, as handled in its Internet Explorer
for Windows 95 and NT. Includes demos.
URL(s)   http://www.microsoft.com/truetype/css/gallery/
entrance.htm

NAME   **Jonny's Crashcourse In Tables**
PROVIDER   Jonny Webhead (Webhead@Webhelp.org)
DESCRIPTION   Short but punchy tutorial on tables.
URL(s)   http://home.tampabay.rr.com/webhelp/tables/

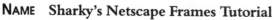

NAME **Sharky's Netscape Frames Tutorial**
PROVIDER Sharky's Solutions
DESCRIPTION Five lesson tutorial on frames.
> **URL(s)** http://www.newbie.net/sharky/frames/menu.html

NAME **Web Style Sheets**
PROVIDER W3C
DESCRIPTION Definitive guide to the development, current standard for and future prospects of cascading style sheets (CSS).
> **URL(s)** http://www.w3.org/Style/

Checking Web pages

NAME **BABEL – Internationalization of the Internet**
PROVIDER Alis Technologies Inc.
DESCRIPTION Multilingual site that uses HTTP's linguistic preference function to determine the language of the page being viewed. The site has information on the world's languages, a typographical and linguistic glossary and plenty of information on developing a multilingual Web site.
> **URL(s)** http://babel.alis.com:8080/index.en.html

NAME **BrowserCaps**
PROVIDER Pragmatic Inc.
DESCRIPTION Designed as a reference tool for Web designers who want to find information on the compatibility of sites and the latest releases of popular browsers and identify which browsers support certain features of HTML. Includes facilities for testing browsers.
> **URL(s)** http://www.browsercaps.com/config/Cv/

Learning HTML

NAME **The Bare Bones Guide to HTML**
PROVIDER Kevin Werbach (barebones@werbach.com)
DESCRIPTION Lists every official HTML tag in common usage, plus the Netscape extensions. At the time of writing it conforms to HTML 3.2 but is being upgraded to the recently-approved HTML 4.0 specification. Available in a large number of languages.
> **URL(s)** http://werbach.com/barebones/

NAME   The Compendium of HTML Elements

PROVIDER   Ron Woodall (nor@synapse.net)

DESCRIPTION   The Compendium is intended as a reference source for users of HTML. At the time of writing, the latest revision includes the Microsoft Internet Explorer 5.0 updates.

> **URL(s)**   http://www.highway57.co.uk/html_ref/sitemap.
> htm (without frames)
> http://www.highway57.co.uk/html_ref/
> mainfram.htm (with frames)
> http://www.htmlcompendium.org/

NAME   Creating HTML – a simple guide

PROVIDER   Jason Borneman (jason.d.borneman@rose-hulman.edu)

DESCRIPTION   A simple, concise guide to writing HTML. This is a site that beginners can use to become familiar with HTML. Available as a compressed file for both PCs and Macs.

> **URL(s)**   http://www.netusa1.net/~jbornema/html.html

NAME   How do they do that with HTML?

PROVIDER   Carl Tashian (carl@tashian.com)

DESCRIPTION   Attempts to be a comprehensive listing of HTML tips and tricks. There are two sections: the first covers the graphics, while the second focuses on HTML. Includes a chat and message board.

> **URL(s)**   http://www.nashville.net/~carl/htmlguide/index.
> html

NAME   HTML – An Interactive Tutorial For Beginners

PROVIDER   Dave Kristula (Webmaster@davesite.com)

DESCRIPTION   A hands-on tutorial that requires the use of either Netscape 2.0 or Microsoft Internet Explorer 2.0 or higher. The idea is to build Web pages while working through the tutorial. There are two levels of tutorial, beginner and advanced, as well as some links to further sources of guidance on HTML.

> **URL(s)**   http://www.davesite.com/webstation/html/

NAME   HTML Help by the Web Design Group

PROVIDER   Web Design Group

DESCRIPTION   Includes help with using both the 3.2 and 4.0 version of HTML, tips on Web design, tools to use and links to other sources of help. Includes a bulletin board system for online help.

> **URL(s)**   http://www.htmlhelp.com/

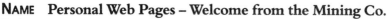

NAME   **Personal Web Pages – Welcome from the Mining Co.**
PROVIDER   General Internet Inc.
DESCRIPTION   While this site has the standard help information on HTML it has lots of useful tips (and examples) for all sorts of personal Web pages (e.g. Web pages for children). Includes chat and a bulletin board.
     URL(s)   http://personalweb.miningco.com/

NAME   **HTML Tutorial**
PROVIDER   Suzanne Cook
DESCRIPTION   Intended to help students at Weber State University make their first World Wide Web pages. It is also a brief guide for beginners.
     URL(s)   http://cs.weber.edu/tutorial/

NAME   **Writing for the Web – a Primer for Librarians**
PROVIDER   Eric Schnell (schnell.9@osu.edu)
DESCRIPTION   The creation and maintenance of Web documents and resources is the most time consuming aspect of managing a library World Wide Web service. This document is not an in-depth HTML guide, it is instead a general introduction to Web resource creation. A glossary of terms associated with the Web is also included.
     URL(s)   http://bones.med.ohio-state.edu/eric/papers/
                      primer/webdocs.html

Style guides

NAME   **Composing Good HTML**
PROVIDER   Eric Tilton (tilt+@cs.cmu.edu)
DESCRIPTION   Divided into two main sections. The first discusses good practices to follow in creating documents, common errors and things to avoid when composing HTML, and, finally, a brief treatment of style sheets. The second section discusses style issues regarding a Web site as a whole, how it is divided and organized, how it is interlinked.
     URL(s)   http://www.cs.cmu.edu/~tilt/cgh/

NAME   **Guide to Web Style**

PROVIDER   Sun Microsystems Inc.

DESCRIPTION   A cookbook for helping people to create better Web pages. The guidelines presented here represent the opinions and preferences of a small group of people within Sun Microsystems who have drawn from their own observations, opinions and judgements about what makes Web pages better or worse, as well as considering usability and user interface design literature. Includes a version designed for printing.

      URL(s)   http://www.sun.com/styleguide/

NAME   **The HTML Author's Board**

PROVIDER   Andreas Waltenspiel (aw@tnet.de)

DESCRIPTION   Has a good list of links to styles guides, and a message board for discussing style and design issues.

      URL(s)   http://homer.touch.net/~aw/hab/

NAME   **Style Guide for Online Hypertext**

PROVIDER   W3C

DESCRIPTION   An early style guide, last updated in 1997, which has not kept pace with developments in HTML, but nevertheless is still worth consulting.

      URL(s)   http://www.w3.org/Provider/Style/Overview.html

NAME   **Tips, Tricks, How To and Beyond**

PROVIDER   Im Biz Co.

DESCRIPTION   Covers a lot of ground, offering solutions to common HTML problems, design and style questions, plus more advanced topics. Has a message board.

      URL(s)   http://tips-tricks.com/

NAME   **Yale C/AIM Style Guide**

PROVIDER   Patrick Lynch (patrick.lynch@yale.edu) and Sarah Horton (sarah.horton@dartmouth.edu)

DESCRIPTION   Generally regarded as the classic, definitive style manual. Available for download in PDF (portable document format).

      URL(s)   http://mirrored.ukoln.ac.uk/Web-authoring/
                       caim/caim/
                       http://info.med.yale.edu/caim/manual/index.html

Web page graphics

NAME **Bandwith Conservation Society**
PROVIDER Infohiway
DESCRIPTION Gives tips on how to optimize graphics for fast download
     URL(s) http://www.infohiway.com/faster/

NAME **Clip Art Searcher**
PROVIDER Internet Advertising
DESCRIPTION Provides search boxes for a range of search engines specializing in clip art. Includes links to sources for backgrounds, bullets, GIF animations and even sound files.
     URL(s) http://www.webplaces.com/search/

NAME **Graphic Arts Us**
PROVIDER Graphic Arts Us
DESCRIPTION Site contains backgrounds and textures, photos and fonts, as well as clip art.
     URL(s) http://www.graphicsrus.com/download/

NAME **IconBazaar**
PROVIDER IconBazaar
DESCRIPTION Enormous collection of clip art, with a simple indexing system for retrieval. Please read the FAQ for restrictions on the use of images.
     URL(s) http://www.iconbazaar.com/

NAME **JPEG FAQ**
PROVIDER Tom Lane (tgl@netcom.com)
DESCRIPTION FAQ about the JPEG image format.
     URL(s) http://www.lib.ox.ac.uk/internet/news/faq/archive/jpeg-faq.part1.html
              http://www.lib.ox.ac.uk/internet/news/faq/archive/jpeg-faq.part2.html
              http://www.cis.ohio-state.edu/hypertext/faq/usenet/jpeg-faq/top.html

NAME MediaBuilder

PROVIDER Andover.Net

DESCRIPTION Both an impressive collection of images and also perhaps the best collection of software downloads for image processing. Some nifty online tools: Animated Banner Maker, ButtonMaker and FontMapper

URL(S) http://www.mediabuilder.com/

Text and background colours

NAME RGBtoHex

PROVIDER Laura Lemay and Eric Murray

DESCRIPTION RGBtoHex converts standard red, green, blue values (three 0 to 255 ASCII numbers indicating red, green and blue) into a hexadecimal triplet that can be used for the background and text colours.

URL(S) http://www.lne.com/rgb.html

NAME The background FAQ

PROVIDER Mark Koenen (markko@sci.kun.nl)

DESCRIPTION Lots of information relating to backgrounds.

URL(S) http://www.sci.kun.nl/thalia/guide/color/faq.html

Sound and video on Web pages

NAME Index to Multimedia Sources

PROVIDER Simon Gibbs (Simon.Gibbs@gmd.de) and Gabor Szentivanyi (szenti@is.twi.tudelft.nl)

DESCRIPTION Includes links to just about everything relevant to multimedia, including FAQs, guides, tutorials, software, archives and more.

URL(S) http://viswiz.gmd.de/MultimediaInfo/

NAME MP3.com

PROVIDER Zoo Inc.

DESCRIPTION Definitive site for the popular MP3 (MPEG 3) format, with links to music, software and hardware devices. Includes a message board.

URL(S) http://www.mp3.com/

NAME The World Wide Web Virtual Library – Audio

PROVIDER Jonathan Bowen (J.P.Bowen@reading.ac.uk)

DESCRIPTION Impressive site with many links to audio archives, relevant software, online radio and numerous FAQs.

URL(S) http://www.comlab.ox.ac.uk/archive/audio.html

NAME Yahoo! UK & Ireland – Sound
PROVIDER Yahoo! Inc.
DESCRIPTION Plenty of links to sound archives.
  URL(s)   http://www.yahoo.co.uk/Computers_and_
         Internet/Multimedia/Sound/

NAME Yahoo! UK & Ireland – Video
PROVIDER Yahoo! Inc.
DESCRIPTION Links to video archives (called 'Collections' for some reason) and information on MPEG and Quicktime video formats.
  URL(s)   http://www.yahoo.co.uk/Computers_and_
         Internet/Multimedia/Video/

NAME Macromedia
PROVIDER Macromedia Inc.
DESCRIPTION Site for Macromedia's Shockwave format and authoring software for it.
  URL(s)   http://www-euro.macromedia.com/
         http://www.macromedia.com/

NAME RealNetworks
PROVIDER RealNetworks Inc.
DESCRIPTION Information on RealNetwork's streaming products.
  URL(s)   http://europe.real.com/
         http://www.realaudio.com/

NAME Videomaker Magazine's Video Streaming FAQ
PROVIDER Videomaker Inc.
DESCRIPTION Extremely useful FAQ on video streaming.
  URL(s)   http://www.streamingvideos.com/strmhome.html

NAME Synchronized Multimedia Integration Language
PROVIDER W3C
DESCRIPTION The standard for SMIL (1.0)
  URL(s)   http://www.w3.org/TR/REC-smil/

NAME The VRML Repository
PROVIDER San Diego Supercomputer Center
DESCRIPTION Contains information on everything related to VRML, including software tools for world building, example applications, object libraries and more.
      URL(s)   http://www.embl-heidelberg.de/vrml/
                        http://www.sdsc.edu/vrml/

Data files and software on Web pages

NAME   Download Free Microsoft Software
PROVIDER Microsoft
DESCRIPTION   Contains downloadable viewers for Word, Excel and Powerpoint files.
      URL(s)   http://www.microsoft.com/msdownload/default.
                        htm#viewers

NAME   Common Internet File Formats
PROVIDER Eric Perlman and Ian Kallen for Internet Literacy Consultants
DESCRIPTION List of file types, and associated player/decompressor software, for both PCs running versions of Windows and Macintoshes.
      URL(s)   http://www.matisse.net/files/formats.html

Interactive Web pages

NAME   Web Communications Forms Tutorial
PROVIDER Web Communications
DESCRIPTION   Solid tutorial on using forms.
      URL(s)   http://www.webcom.com/~webcom/html/tutor/
                        forms/

NAME   Intranet Software Catalog
PROVIDER Innergy Inc.
DESCRIPTION   Excellent listing of middleware and database gateway products.
      URL(s)   http://www.innergy.com/tools.shtml#Head

NAME   Site Search Tools

PROVIDER   Search Tools Consulting and Avi Rappoport

DESCRIPTION   Contains a product listing of site search tools, reviews, current news etc. Offers a free newsletter.

URL(s)   http://www.searchtools.com/searchtools.html

Chapter 4
DESIGNING WEB SITES

Basic design

NAME   Adobe Acrobat
PROVIDER   Adobe Systems Inc.
DESCRIPTION   Source for information on the Acrobat format, software, case studies etc.
>   **URL(s)**   http://www.adobe.com/prodindex/acrobat/main. html

NAME   Good Documents
PROVIDER   Trellix Corporation
DESCRIPTION   Discusses how to create good business documents in the linked, onscreen Web environment. Offers advice on design techniques and examples. A mailing list is used for updates.
>   **URL(s)**   http://www.gooddocuments.com/homepage/ homepage.htm

NAME   Alertbox: Current Issues in Web Usability
PROVIDER   Jakob Nielsen
DESCRIPTION   A regular column by Jakob Nielsen, a Web usability 'guru'. Always an interesting read: some are classics. Notifications of a new column can be e-mailed.
>   **URL(s)**   http://www.useit.com/alertbox/

NAME   Improving Web Site Usability and Appeal
PROVIDER   Microsoft
DESCRIPTION   A set of guidelines compiled by Microsoft Network (MSN) Usability Research. Available for downloading as a Word document.
>   **URL(s)**   http://www.microsoft.com/workshop/ management/planning/improvingsiteusa.asp

NAME   **Usable Web**

PROVIDER   Keith Instone (instone@usableWeb.com)

DESCRIPTION   The source for Web usability information. A well-structured set of links lead to information on design issues, Web technology, conferences, courses, other information sources etc.

URL(s)   http://usableweb.com/

NAME   **Web pages that suck**

PROVIDER   Vincent Flanders

DESCRIPTION   How not to do it. Some very amusing examples of disastrous Web pages.

URL(s)   http://www.webpagesthatsuck.com/home.html

NAME   **Web Design – Welcome from the Mining Co.**

PROVIDER   General Internet Inc.

DESCRIPTION   Perhaps the best of the Mining Company Web-related sites. A well-structured list of subsections is offered, covering design and related technical issues. An e-mail newsletter announces updates. There is chat and a discussion board.

URL(s)   http://webdesign.miningco.com/

NAME   **Web Design & Review**

PROVIDER   The Design & Publishing Center

DESCRIPTION   Eclectic but interesting irregular magazine on design issues. Available for download in PDF format.

URL(s)   http://www.graphic-design.com/Web/Default.html

File structures and links

NAME   **Image Map Authoring Guide and Tutorial Sites**

PROVIDER   Automata

DESCRIPTION   Good listing of tutorial sites for image maps

URL(s)   http://www.cris.com/%7Eautomata/tutorial.shtml

NAME   **Imagemap Help Page**

PROVIDER   Steve Rogers (Webmaster@ihip.com)

DESCRIPTION   Short and simple to follow tutorial.

URL(s)   http://www.ihip.com/

Chapter 5
PUBLISHING WEB SITES

The basics of publishing a Web site

NAME W3C HTML Validation Service
PROVIDER W3C
DESCRIPTION An easy-to-use HTML validation service based on an SGML parser. It checks HTML documents for compliance with HTML 4.0.
      URL(S)   http://validator.w3.org/

NAME W3C CSS Validation Service
PROVIDER W3C
DESCRIPTION Validates HTML with CSS or CSS only.
      URL(S)   http://jigsaw.w3.org/css-validator/
                          validator-uri.html

NAME Best Viewed with Any Browser
PROVIDER Cari D. Burstein (campaign@anybrowser.org)
DESCRIPTION Launches with a quote from Berners-Lee decrying proprietary browser tags. Very much a campaigning site although it links to many useful Web design resources and is available in numerous language translations.
      URL(S)   http://www.anybrowser.org/campaign/

NAME Bobby
PROVIDER CAST (Center for Applied Special Technology)
DESCRIPTION Bobby is an HTML validator that will also analyse Web pages for their accessibility to people with disabilities.
      URL(S)   http://www.cast.org/bobby/

NAME **WAI Accessibility Guidelines: Page Authoring**

PROVIDER W3C

DESCRIPTION A list of markup guidelines that HTML authors should follow in order to make their pages more accessible for people with disabilities and more useful to indexing robots.

URL(s) http://www.w3.org/TR/WD-WAI-PAGEAUTH

NAME **Yahoo! UK & Ireland – HTML Validators and Checkers**

PROVIDER Yahoo! Inc.

DESCRIPTION A comprehensive list of HTML validators.

URL(s) http://www.yahoo.co.uk/Computers_and_
Internet/Information_and_Documentation/
Data_Formats/HTML/Validation_and_Checkers/

NAME **NetMechanic**

PROVIDER Monte Sano Software

DESCRIPTION A service that checks Web sites to find broken links, performs HTML validation, optimizes images and monitors server performance.

URL(s) http://www.netmechanic.com/

NAME **Web Site Garage**

PROVIDER AtWeb Inc.

DESCRIPTION Offers a unique range of services: performance diagnostics of a Web site, testing browser compatibility, an image optimizer and a site traffic tracking tool. However, most services are available only after signing on for a free newsletter.

URL(s) http://www.websitegarage.com/

Web servers

NAME **The List**

PROVIDER Mecklermedia

DESCRIPTION Attempts to be the definitive guide to Internet Service Providers (ISP), those companies that provide access to the Internet. ISPs are listed by country, with most coverage in the USA.

URL(s) http://thelist.internet.com/

NAME **budgetWeb.com**
PROVIDER budgetWeb.com
DESCRIPTION Gives a listing of cheaper Web space providers, broken down by those giving virtual or non-virtual domains. Useful information about how to set up a Web site is also given, together with some interesting links. There is information on scanning and design services.
       URL(s) http://www.budgetweb.com/budgetweb/index. html

NAME **Choosing a Web Host**
PROVIDER andrew@serve.com
DESCRIPTION Page giving a handy checklist of features to look for when choosing a Web host.
       URL(s) http://www.serve.com/andrew/

NAME **Top Hosts**
PROVIDER Top Hosts
DESCRIPTION Offers a searchable database of over 500 hosts along with a ranking of the top 15 hosts. Mainly US-based hosts included.
       URL(s) http://www.tophosts.com/

NAME **The Ultimate Web Host list**
PROVIDER Sumo Inc.
DESCRIPTION Gives a top 25 listing of Web hosts, chosen by a review panel. There is also a large listing of Web hosts and a list of Web designers.
       URL(s) http://www.webhostlist.com/

NAME **Free Homepage Center**
PROVIDER FHCenter@usa.net
DESCRIPTION Lists sources of free Web space, and also other free services (e-mail etc.) available via the Web.
       URL(s) http://www.freehomepage.com/main.htm

NAME **ServerStats.com**
PROVIDER Addy & Associates, Inc.
DESCRIPTION Runs a regular survey and analysis of the software used to run Web servers on the Internet.
       URL(s) http://serverstats.com/

NAME WebServer Compare

PROVIDER Mecklermedia Corporation

DESCRIPTION A comprehensive guide to Web server software. It allows searches for server software matching a wide range of criteria.

> **URL(s)** http://webcompare.internet.com/

Web site promotion

NAME Search Engine Watch

PROVIDER Danny Sullivan

DESCRIPTION The one source to go to for any information relating to search engines. Its 'Guide for webmasters' is particularly useful in learning how to promote a Web site. Offers an e-mail newsletter.

> **URL(s)** http://searchenginewatch.com/

NAME Add Me!

PROVIDER Add Me! Inc.

DESCRIPTION Submits details of a site to 34 popular search engines

> **URL(s)** http://www.addme.com/

NAME Report Dead Links to the Major Search Engines

PROVIDER gmik@uconect.net

DESCRIPTION Unlike the usual submission services, this one links to URL removal pages at search engine databases.

> **URL(s)** http://www.uconect.net/~gmik/dead-link-
> remover.htm

NAME Broadcaster

PROVIDER PlanetWeb Systems Ltd

DESCRIPTION The only one of the best submission services to be based in the UK.

> **URL(s)** http://www.broadcaster.co.uk/

NAME FAQ: How to Announce your new Web Site

PROVIDER EPage

DESCRIPTION Contains some useful tips on places to promote a Web site. Although this FAQ is posted regularly to the newsgroup comp.infosystems.www.announce it is, however, somewhat dated.

> **URL(s)** http://ep.com/faq/webannounce.html

NAME   PositionAgent

PROVIDER Submit It! Inc.

DESCRIPTION   PositionAgent monitors Web site rankings in the search engines. There is a free service and a more sophisticated one for members. A newsletter with the latest ranking tips is available.

> **URL(s)**   http://www.positionagent.com/

NAME   Submit It!

PROVIDER Submit It! Inc.

DESCRIPTION   The principal service for announcing a Web site to a selection of more than 400 search engines, directories, what's new sites and award sites.

> **URL(s)**   http://www.submit-it.com/

NAME   Robot Exclusion

PROVIDER Martijn Koster (m.koster@Webcrawler.com)

DESCRIPTION   Details the two ways to indicate which parts of a Web site should not be visited by a robot, by providing a specially formatted file, in 'http://.../robots.txt' and by the use of a special HTML Meta tag.

> **URL(s)**   http://info.webcrawler.com/mak/projects/robots/
> exclusion.html

NAME   RankThis!

PROVIDER WebPromote

DESCRIPTION   RankThis! determines a Web page's 'ranking' on different keyword sets in ten of the major search engines. It will list the sites that are in the top ten for that keyword set. There is a guide to improving rankings and a discussion group for help.

> **URL(s)**   http://www.rankthis.com/

NAME   Yahoo! UK & Ireland – Banner Exchanges

PROVIDER Yahoo! Inc.

DESCRIPTION   A comprehensive list of banner exchanges.

> **URL(s)**   http://www.yahoo.co.uk/Computers_and_
> Internet/
> Internet/World_Wide_Web/Announcement_
> Services/
> Banner_Exchanges/

NAME Welcome to WebRing!
PROVIDER Starseed Inc.
DESCRIPTION Lists Web rings, both by browsable topic and by keyword search.
     URL(S)   http://www.webring.org/

Usage tracking

NAME Analog
PROVIDER Stephen Turner (sret1@cam.ac.uk)
DESCRIPTION Analog is a program that analyses the logfiles from Web servers. It reveals which pages are most popular, from which sites people are visiting, from sites they tried to follow broken links, etc.
     URL(S)   http://www.statslab.cam.ac.uk/~sret1/analog/

NAME Counters, Counters, Counters!
PROVIDER counters@merlet.com
DESCRIPTION This site contains links to hundreds of sites offering Web page counters and other types of statistical service.
     URL(S)   http://www.merlet.com/counterlinks.htm

NAME Non-CGI Access Log Unofficial FAQ
PROVIDER Tim Drozinski (tdroz@earthlink.net)
DESCRIPTION This FAQ is for those who are unable to use CGI scripts in their Web pages to obtain hit counts.
     URL(S)   http://erau.db.erau.edu/~tjd/log_faq.html

NAME Cookie Central
PROVIDER Cookie Central
DESCRIPTION Dedicated to providing full information on cookies, it includes a FAQ with basic information and links to other cookie resources.
     URL(S)   http://www.cookiecentral.com/

NAME HTTP Cookie Info
PROVIDER Andy Kington (andy@macpac.com)
DESCRIPTION Excellent guide to using cookies.
     URL(S)   http://www.illuminatus.com/cookie.fcgi

NAME   **Platform for Privacy Preferences (P3P) Project**
PROVIDER   W3C
DESCRIPTION   Platform for Privacy Preferences P3P Project specification.
      URL(s)   http://www.w3.org/P3P/

Social and legal issues

NAME   **Platform for Internet Content Selection**
PROVIDER   W3C
DESCRIPTION   Links to the specification for PICs and related information.
      URL(s)   http://www.w3.org/PICS/

NAME   **Sex, Censorship and the Internet**
PROVIDER   Carl M. Kadie (kadie@eff.org)
DESCRIPTION   Thought-provoking collection of case studies illustrating various issues in Internet control.
      URL(s)   http://www.eff.org/CAF/cafuiuc.html

NAME   **Welcome to Netparents.org**
PROVIDER   Netparents.org
DESCRIPTION   A guide to resources for parents who want to protect their children from inappropriate material online. A neutral approach is taken; there is no endorsement of any one product or approach over another.
      URL(s)   http://www.netparents.org/

NAME   **Web Law FAQ**
PROVIDER   Oppedahl & Larson
DESCRIPTION   Excellent guide to copyright law as it affects materials on the World Wide Web.
      URL(s)   http://www.patents.com/weblaw.sht

NAME   **The World Wide Web Security FAQ**
PROVIDER   W3C
DESCRIPTION   Definitive listing of known security problems relating to the World Wide Web.
      URL(s)   http://www.man.ac.uk/~mbzalgd/www-security/
                http://www.w3.org/Security/faq/www-security-faq.html

Applications of the World Wide Web

NAME Conferencing Software for the Web
PROVIDER David R. Woolley
DESCRIPTION Comprehensive listing of free and commercial Web conferencing software, together with product reviews and news.
URL(s) http://thinkofit.com/webconf/

NAME Internet Conferencing – Welcome from the Mining Co.
PROVIDER General Internet Inc.
DESCRIPTION Very expansive list of resources, both on general topics such as video conferencing and netiquette, and on specific 'chat' software tools, for example, ICQ and PowWow.
URL(s) http://netconference.miningco.com/

NAME CSCW & Groupware Index
PROVIDER Diamond Bullet Design
DESCRIPTION Focus is very strongly on groupware, with many links to papers, conferences etc. on this topic.
URL(s) http://www.usabilityfirst.com/cscw.html

NAME Democracies Online
PROVIDER Steven Clift
DESCRIPTION This site aims to promote the development of online civic participation and democracy efforts around the world.
URL(s) http://www.e-democracy.org/do/

NAME Governments on WWW
PROVIDER Gunnar Anzinger (a@gksoft.com)
DESCRIPTION Listing of thousands of governmental institutions on the World Wide Web at all levels of government.
URL(s) http://www.gksoft.com/govt/

NAME CCTA Government Information Service
PROVIDER CCTA
DESCRIPTION Covers offshoots from the government.direct Green Paper and 'direct access government' developments in the UK.
URL(s) http://www.open.gov.uk/

NAME **Association for Interactive Media**
PROVIDER Association for Interactive Media
DESCRIPTION The Association for Interactive Media (AIM) is a non-profit trade association for business users of the Internet. It lobbies governments on behalf of Internet business interests. Offers mailing lists for up to the minute news affecting business on the Internet.
>   **URL(S)**   http://www.interactivehq.org/

NAME **The Industry Standard: the Newsmagazine of the Internet Economy**
PROVIDER Industry Standard
DESCRIPTION Excellent source of news and trends for Internet business. Offers an e-mail newsletter.
>   **URL(S)**   http://www.thestandard.net/

NAME **Internet.com's Electronic Commerce Guide**
PROVIDER Internet.com
DESCRIPTION Offers information about e-commerce in general, particularly e-commerce software packages, e-payment systems and more.
>   **URL(S)**   http://e-comm.internet.com/

NAME **Internet Advertising Bureau**
PROVIDER BDInteractive
DESCRIPTION The Internet Advertising Bureau (IAB) is devoted to maximizing the use and effectiveness of advertising on the Internet. This site contains details of IAB events, advertising research and news.
>   **URL(S)**   http://www.iab.net/

NAME **Professional Presence Network**
PROVIDER WebBranch Internet Marketing
DESCRIPTION Professional Presence Network (PPN) is an organization for Web development professionals that wants to establish standards of excellence in Web design and promotion. This site is a good source of information on current trends in business Web site design. It offers a bulletin board.
>   **URL(S)**   http://www.ppn.org/

NAME **SearchZ: the Ultimate Guide to Online Marketing, Advertising and E-commerce**

PROVIDER ClickZ Corporation

DESCRIPTION The source for e-commerce material. Searchable, and offers links to sites making the running in many areas of business. Also offers a number of conferences.

> **URL(s)**   http://www.searchz.com/index.shtml

NAME **Web Marketing Today Info Center**

PROVIDER Wilson Internet Services

DESCRIPTION A massive site, covering just about everything connected with e-commerce.

> **URL(s)**   http://www.wilsonweb.com/webmarket/

Resources linked to Part II

Chapter 6
LIBRARIES AND THE WORLD WIDE WEB

Academic libraries

NAME   JANET Home Page
PROVIDER   JNT Association
DESCRIPTION   Comprehensive information about the activities and services of JANET, the .ac.uk domain etc.
        URL(s)   http://www.ja.net/

NAME   eLib Programme
PROVIDER   Joint Information Systems Committee (JISC)
DESCRIPTION   Gives a history of the eLib Programme, links to project reports, work in progress etc. There is a particularly insightful summary of eLib by Chris Rushbridge, its Programme Director, called 'Towards the hybrid library' linked to from D-lib magazine.
        URL(s)   http://www.ukoln.ac.uk/services/elib/

Public libraries

NAME   CLIP: Croydon Libraries Internet Project
PROVIDER   The British Library Board
DESCRIPTION   HTML version of the final report of CLIP as presented to the British Library.
        URL(s)   http://www.croydon.gov.uk/cr-cliphtml.htm

NAME   IT Point
PROVIDER   IT Point
DESCRIPTION   Contains a report about the IT Point Project, as well as related projects based at Solihull Libraries.
        URL(s)   http://www.itpoint.org.uk/home.html

NAME Library and Information Commission public library Internet survey

PROVIDER UKOLN

DESCRIPTION Reports on a survey carried out by UKOLN on public library Internet use in 1995.

> **URL(s)** http://www.ukoln.ac.uk/services/papers/ukoln/ ormes-1995-01/

NAME EARL: the Consortium for Public Library networking

PROVIDER EARL

DESCRIPTION The EARL Consortium of UK public libraries and associated organizations was established in 1995 to aid public libraries in providing library and information services via the Internet. EARL now has over 140 partners from local public library authorities and other related organizations, and has established 16 task Groups to focus on specific areas.

> **URL(s)** http://www.earl.org.uk/

NAME New Library: the People's Network

PROVIDER Library and Information Commission

DESCRIPTION Influential report that attempts to find a role for libraries in networked information and argues for government support to enable them to take up this new challenge.

> **URL(s)** http://www.ukoln.ac.uk/services/lic/newlibrary/

Special libraries and information units

NAME Shell International

PROVIDER Shell International

DESCRIPTION Corporate Web site distinguished by a strong library presence in disseminating information about the company.

> **URL(s)** http://www.shell.com/

NAME BUBL Information Service

PROVIDER Joint Information Systems Committee (JISC)

DESCRIPTION BUBL is a national information service for the UK higher education community, which aims to provide access to Internet resources and services of academic, research and professional significance.

> **URL(s)** http://bubl.ac.uk/

NAME   UK Public Libraries on the Web
PROVIDER   Sheila and Robert Harden
DESCRIPTION   A complete listing of UK public library services accessible via the Internet.
URL(s)   http://dspace.dial.pipex.com/town/square/ac940/weblibs.html

NAME   NISS
PROVIDER   Joint Information Systems Committee (JISC)
DESCRIPTION   NISS provides a focal point for the UK education and research communities to access information resources on the Internet.
URL(s)   http://www.niss.ac.uk/

NAME   UKOLN
PROVIDER   Joint Information Systems Committee (JISC) and The British Library Research and Innovation Centre (BLRIC)
DESCRIPTION   UKOLN is the UK national centre for awareness, research and information services in network information management in the library and information communities.
URL(s)   http://www.ukoln.ac.uk/

NAME   Library Land
PROVIDER   Jerry Kuntz (jkuntz@rcls.org)
DESCRIPTION   Excellent resource for library-related information.
URL(s)   http://www.rcls.org/libland/

Chapter 7
WORLD WIDE WEB APPLICATIONS IN LIBRARIES

Public relations, promotion and sales

NAME   Project EARL Policy Issues/Public Access Strategies Task Group
PROVIDER   EARL
DESCRIPTION   EARL task group working to to assist public library authorities to develop public access strategies and establish roles for library services in networked information.

URL(s)   http://www.walsplsm.demon.co.uk/

NAME   North Lincolnshire Libraries
PROVIDER   North Lincolnshire Libraries and Information Services
DESCRIPTION   This well-designed site shows what services North Lincolnshire Libraries offer their users (lending, information services, etc.).

URL(s)   http://www.btwebworld.com/northlincs/library/index.htm

NAME   City of Leeds: Library and Information Services
PROVIDER   Leeds Library and Information Services
DESCRIPTION   A rather densely-packed tabular site that puts across a lot of information regarding Leeds Library services.

URL(s)   http://www.leeds.gov.uk/library/library.html

NAME   **Essex Libraries**
PROVIDER   Essex County Council
DESCRIPTION   Very nice image map of a pile of books for the main links and other image links for certain services. Also textual equivalent links for those not viewing images in their browser.
>   **URL(s)**   http://www.essexcc.gov.uk/infoserv/ecc_lib/essex.htm

NAME   **Nottinghamshire County Council Library Services**
PROVIDER   Nottinghamshire County Council
DESCRIPTION   Plain page consisting of a large imagemap (depicting a library) with just the main links to services and also textual link equivalents.
>   **URL(s)**   http://www.nottscc.gov.uk/libraries/

User queries, participation and feedback

NAME   **IPL Ask a Question Form**
PROVIDER   School of Information, University of Michigan (USA)
DESCRIPTION   The Internet Public Library (IPL) provides links to Internet resources. Its 'Ask a question' service requires that questions must be reference rather than research orientated. Uses a rather long but comprehensive form to build a picture of the question and its background.
>   **URL(s)**
>   http://ipl.ub.lu.se/ref/QUE/RefFormQRC.html
>   http://www.ipl.org/ref/QUE/ RefFormQRC.html

NAME   **Ask a Librarian.**
PROVIDER   EARL.
DESCRIPTION   Allows the public to e-mail a question and receive a response within two days. It is aimed at answering factual questions (unsurprisingly) and is visited frequently. Very simple question form.
>   **URL(s)**   http://www.earl.org.uk/ask/index.html

NAME   **The Library Web Manager's Reference Center**
PROVIDER   The Library, UC Berkeley and Sun Microsystems Inc.
DESCRIPTION   The best site for librarians looking for technical information and help related to library functions on the Web. Source of library-related forms, CGI scripts, solutions for particular technical problems, tutorials, online books and more. Archive of the excellent 'Web4Lib' mailing list, another vital resource when applying the Web in libraries.
URL(s)   http://sunsite.berkeley.edu/web4Lib/faq.html

Training and instruction

NAME   **Netskills**
PROVIDER   Joint Information Systems Committee (JISC)
DESCRIPTION   Netskills helps the UK higher education community to develop the skills to make effective use of the Internet. You must register before being able to browse the training materials. A fee may be required for their use.
URL(s)   http://www.netskills.ac.uk/

NAME   **NetLearn**
PROVIDER   Iain A. Middleton (i.middleton@rgu.ac.uk)
DESCRIPTION   NetLearn is a vast directory of resources for learning and teaching all kinds of Internet skills. Recommended for the trainer.
URL(s)   http://www.rgu.ac.uk/~sim/research/netlearn/
             callist.htm

Library databases

NAME   **SALSER**
PROVIDER   EDINA (Edinburgh Data and Information Access)
DESCRIPTION   SALSER is a Web-based union catalogue of serials holdings in all Scottish universities, the National Library of Scotland and the larger municipal research libraries.
URL(s)   http://edina.ed.ac.uk/salser

NAME   **Initiatives for Access**
PROVIDER   British Library
DESCRIPTION   The Initiatives for Access Programme has now been subsumed in the British Library's Digital Library Programme which aims to enable the Library to use computer technology to preserve and extend access to its collection.
URL(s)   http://www.bl.uk/diglib/access/

NAME **American Memory**
PROVIDER Library of Congress
DESCRIPTION The National Digital Library Program is an effort to digitize and deliver by network the distinctive, historical Americana holdings at the Library of Congress. The American Memory Historical Collections are a component of this source.
   URL(s) http://memory.loc.gov/ammem/

NAME **The University of Houston Libraries' Special Collections on the Web**
PROVIDER Julie Grob (julie@jetson.uh.edu)
DESCRIPTION This page links to archival and library associations: indexes of rare book dealers, preservation resources etc. that are of interest and use to archivists, special collections librarians and scholars.
   URL(s) http://info.lib.uh.edu/speccoll/specoWeb.htm

Leased databases

NAME **BIDS: Bath Information & Data Services**
PROVIDER Bath Information & Data Services
DESCRIPTION BIDS is a UK provider of networked information services for higher education and research, which offers key bibliographic databases.
   URL(s) http://www.bids.ac.uk/

NAME **OCLC FirstSearch**
PROVIDER OCLC (Online Computer Library Center)
DESCRIPTION The OCLC FirstSearch service gives users access to a large number of online databases and millions of full-text articles.
   URL(s) http://www.oclc.org/oclc/menu/fs.htm

NAME **MEDLINE**
PROVIDER National Library of Medicine
DESCRIPTION Enormous bibliographic database covering the fields of medicine, nursing, dentistry, veterinary medicine, the health care system and the preclinical sciences.
   URL(s) http://www.nlm.nih.gov/databases/medline.html

NAME EBSCO
PROVIDER EBSCO Information Services
DESCRIPTION EBSCO provides integrated serials access and delivery via subscription management, online access and document delivery.
      URL(s) http://www-uk.ebsco.com/home/
                http://www.ebsco.com/home/

NAME Dialog Web
PROVIDER The Dialog Corporation
DESCRIPTION Web-accessible verion of DIALOG.
      URL(s) http://www.dialogweb.com/

NAME Ovid
PROVIDER Ovid Technologies
DESCRIPTION Forward-looking commercial service providing access to a wide range of bibliographic and live full text databases for academic, biomedical and scientific research.
      URL(s) http://www.ovid.com/

NAME MIAMILINK
PROVIDER Miami University Libraries
DESCRIPTION Superb example of a local library gateway linking to a wide range of searchable resources.
      URL(s) http://www.lib.muohio.edu/

Links to other Internet resources

NAME South Ayrshire Council: Libraries & Information Services
PROVIDER South Ayrshire Council
DESCRIPTION Award-winning collection of links, well thought out and structured.
      URL(s) http://www.south-ayrshire.gov.uk/

NAME BUBL Link
PROVIDER BUBL
DESCRIPTION Carefully selected collection of resources, browsable by subject and Dewey number, and keyword searchable.
      URL(s) http://bubl.ac.uk/link/

NAME EARLWeb
PROVIDER EARL
DESCRIPTION A collection of resources under a few general headings: searchable.
URL(s) http://www.earl.org.uk/earlweb/index.html

NAME ADAM
PROVIDER ADAM
DESCRIPTION ADAM (Art, Design, Architecture & Media Information Gateway) is a collection of digital art, design, architecture and media Internet resources.
URL(s) http://adam.ac.uk/

NAME Biz/ed
PROVIDER Biz/ed
DESCRIPTION Biz/ed is a dedicated business and economics information gateway.
URL(s) http://www.bizednet.bris.ac.uk:8080/

NAME Business information sources on the Internet
PROVIDER Sheila Webber
DESCRIPTION Superb collection of resources pertaining to business.
URL(s) http://www.dis.strath.ac.uk/business/index.html

NAME ChemDex
PROVIDER Mark Winter
DESCRIPTION A directory of chemistry resources on the Internet.
URL(s) http://www.shef.ac.uk/~chem/chemdex/

NAME EEVL
PROVIDER Heriot-Watt University Library
DESCRIPTION The Edinburgh Engineering Virtual Library (EEVL) is a gateway to quality engineering information on the Internet.
URL(s) http://eevl.icbl.hw.ac.uk/

NAME ELDIS
PROVIDER Institute of Development Studies
DESCRIPTION The Electronic Development and Environment Information System (ELDIS) links to online documents, organizations and bibliographic information for development studies.
URL(s) http://nt1.ids.ac.uk/eldis/

NAME History
PROVIDER Institute of Historical Research
DESCRIPTION Gateway to Internet resources on history. Has foreign language versions.
        URL(s) http://ihr.sas.ac.uk

NAME HUMBUL
PROVIDER Oxford University
DESCRIPTION HUMBUL (the HUManities BULletin board) was started in the mid 1980s, using bulletin board software. Now it is a Web gateway that leads to quality resources in the humanities.
        URL(s) http://users.ox.ac.uk/~humbul/

NAME OMNI
PROVIDER OMNI Consortium
DESCRIPTION Organising Medical Networked Information (OMNI) is a gateway to high quality biomedical Internet resources.
        URL(s) http://omni.ac.uk/

NAME PICK
PROVIDER Thomas Parry Library, University of Wales Aberystwyth
DESCRIPTION PICK is a gateway to quality librarianship and information science resources on the Internet.
        URL(s) http://www.aber.ac.uk/~tplwww/e/

NAME RUDI
PROVIDER RUDI
DESCRIPTION Resource for Urban Design Information (RUDI) is an information resource for research, teaching and professional practice in the field of urban design.
        URL(s) http://rudi.herts.ac.uk/

NAME SOSIG
PROVIDER SOSIG (Social Sciences Information Gateway)
DESCRIPTION SOSIG is an online catalogue of high quality Internet resources that are relevant to the social sciences.
        URL(s) http://sosig.ac.uk/

NAME **Beyond bookmarks: schemes for organizing the Web**
PROVIDER Gerry McKiernan (gerrymck@iastate.edu)
DESCRIPTION A definitive collection of Web sites that have used standard classification schemes or controlled vocabularies to organize Internet resources.
    URL(S)   http://www.iastate.edu/~CYBERSTACKS/CTW. htm

Filtering

NAME **Internet Filter Assessment Project**
PROVIDER Karen G. Schneider
DESCRIPTION Reports on an investigation into the effectiveness of filters.
    URL(S)   http://www.bluehighways.com/tifap/

NAME **Resolution on the use of filtering software in libraries**
PROVIDER American Library Association (ALA)
DESCRIPTION Clear statement of the ALA's position on filters.
    URL(S)   http://www.ala.org/alaorg/oif/filt_res.html

NAME **Filtering Facts**
PROVIDER David Burt
DESCRIPTION The quintessential pro-filtering site.
    URL(S)   http://www.filteringfacts.org

NAME **Family Friendly Libraries**
PROVIDER Family Friendly Libraries
DESCRIPTION A site that is ardent in its support for filtering.
    URL(S)   http://www.fflibraries.org

Z39.50 and the World Wide Web

NAME **Z39.50 Maintenance Agency**
PROVIDER Library of Congress
DESCRIPTION This page provides information on the development and maintenance of Z39.50 and its implementation.
    URL(S)   http://lcweb.loc.gov/z3950/agency/

Name   **Directory of Z39.50 targets in the UK**
Provider   UKOLN
Description   A directory service that provides information about Z39.50 targets in the UK, supports the configuration of Z39.50 clients and facilitates connection to UK services.

       URL(s)   http://www.ukoln.ac.uk/dlis/zdir/

Resources linked to Part III

Chapter 8
FUNDAMENTAL WEB TECHNOLOGY

HTTP and HTML

NAME HyperText Transfer Protocol – Next Generation Overview
PROVIDER W3C
DESCRIPTION Gives the latest state of the HTTP-NG Project.
      URL(s)   http://www.w3.org/Protocols/HTTP-NG/

NAME Unicode
PROVIDER Unicode Inc.
DESCRIPTION The Unicode Consortium Web site contains information on the Unicode standard.
      URL(s)   http://www.unicode.org/

NAME Document Object Model (DOM)
PROVIDER W3C
DESCRIPTION An overview of DOM-related materials at W3C and on the Web generally.
      URL(s)   http://www.w3.org/DOM/

NAME DHTML, HTML and CSS
PROVIDER Microsoft
DESCRIPTION Microsoft's view of DHTML and its component technologies.
      URL(s)   http://www.microsoft.com/workshop/author/
                         default.asp

NAME   Dynamic HTML Index

PROVIDER   All-links.com

DESCRIPTION   A large and ever-growing collection of links relating to DHTML resources.

   URL(S)   http://www.all-links.com/dynamic/

NAME   Dynamic HTML Zone

PROVIDER   Macromedia

DESCRIPTION   Contains articles, tutorials etc. for DHTML. The site also describes the differences in the approach to DHTML taken by Microsoft and Netscape.

   URL(S)   http://www.dhtmlzone.com/alt.html

NAME   Inside Dynamic HTML

PROVIDER   InsideDHTML.com

DESCRIPTION   A useful site, with an emphasis on listing 'how to do tips' for certain functions using DHTML. Offers a mailing list.

   URL(S)   http://www.insidedhtml.com/home.asp

NAME   Extensible Markup Language (XML) 1.0

PROVIDER   W3C

DESCRIPTION   XML 1.0 specification.

   URL(S)   http://www.w3.org/TR/1998/REC-xml-19980210

NAME   Frequently Asked Questions about the Extensible Markup Language

PROVIDER   Peter Flynn

DESCRIPTION   Superb FAQ, which is the clearest explanation of XML available.

   URL(S)   http://www.ucc.ie/xml/

NAME   The SGML/XML Home Page

PROVIDER   Robin Cover

DESCRIPTION   Rather daunting site containing reference information and software pertaining to the SGML and its subset, the XML.

   URL(S)   http://www.sil.org/sgml/sgml.html

NAME XML.COM
PROVIDER Seybold Publications and O'Reilly & Associates Inc.
DESCRIPTION Excellent collection of information based around a journal on XML.
> **URL(s)**   http://www.xml.com/xml/pub

Resource description

NAME Persistent URL Home Page
PROVIDER OCLC PURL Service
DESCRIPTION Definitive source of information on PURLs.
> **URL(s)**   http://purl.oclc.org/

NAME Web Naming and Addressing Overview
PROVIDER W3C
DESCRIPTION Contains definitions of URIs, URLs, URNs etc.
> **URL(s)**   http://www.w3.org/Addressing/Addressing.html

NAME Universal Resource Identifiers
PROVIDER W3C
DESCRIPTION The URI specification.
> **URL(s)**   http://www.w3.org/Addressing/URL/URI_
> Overview.html

NAME Universal Resource Names
PROVIDER Daniel LaLiberte (liberte@ncsa.uiuc.edu)
DESCRIPTION Information on URNs and name resolution.
> **URL(s)**   http://www.hypernews.org/HyperNews/get/
> www/URNs.html

NAME Universal Resource Characteristics
PROVIDER Daniel LaLiberte (liberte@ncsa.uiuc.edu) and Michael Shapiro (mshapiro@ncsa.uiuc.edu)
DESCRIPTION Information about URCs.
> **URL(s)**   http://www.hypernews.org/HyperNews/get/
> www/URCs.html

NAME Dublin Core Metadata Element Set
PROVIDER OCLC
DESCRIPTION Source for the Dublin Core 15-element metadata element set.
> **URL(s)**   http://purl.oclc.org/metadata/dublin_core/

NAME   **W3C Resource Description Framework**
PROVIDER   W3C
DESCRIPTION   The RDF specification.
       URL(s)   http://www.w3.org/RDF/

Chapter 9
ASSOCIATED WEB TECHNOLOGY

CGI and server-side scripting

NAME Server Side Includes Tutorial
PROVIDER Craig McFetridge
DESCRIPTION Basic tutorial on server side includes.
    URL(s)   http://www.carleton.ca/~dmcfet/html/ssi.html

NAME Active Server Pages Site
PROVIDER Aspsite.com
DESCRIPTION Good source on active server pages, an adjunct to a book on the topic. Offers a discussion board.
    URL(s)   http://www.aspsite.com/

NAME Web-Database Gateways
PROVIDER letovsky@gdb.org
DESCRIPTION Excellent listing of products, with links to other sites.
    URL(s)   http://gdbdoc.gdb.org/letovsky/genera/dbgw.html

NAME PERL.COM
PROVIDER O'Reilly & Associates Inc.
DESCRIPTION One-stop source for information on PERL. Downloadable PERL software, journals, information on all applications of PERL and more. Offers a number of discussion boards.
    URL(s)   http://www.perl.com/pace/pub

NAME   **PERL CGI Programming FAQ**
PROVIDER   Shishir Gundavaram (shishir@ora.com) and Tom Christiansen
(tchrist@perl.com)
DESCRIPTION   Excellent source for an introduction to PERL.
URL(s)   http://www.perl.com/CPAN-local/doc/
FAQs/cgi/perl-cgi-faq.html

NAME   **CGI Resource Index**
PROVIDER   Matt's Script Archive, Inc.
DESCRIPTION   Chiefly a big collection of links to program scripts (not all in
PERL), but there are also lists of books, journal articles and even PERL
programmers. Companion site to *Matt's Script Archive* (below).
URL(s)   http://www.cgi-resources.com/

NAME   **Matt's Script Archive**
PROVIDER   Matt's Script Archive Inc.
DESCRIPTION   Excellent listing of PERL scripts by function, with informa-
tion and documentation on each one. Companion site to the *CGI Resource
Index* (above).
URL(s)   http://worldwidemart.com/scripts/

NAME   **Scripting news**
PROVIDER   dave@scripting.com
DESCRIPTION   Useful journal looking at scripting in general. Archive of back
copies available for searching.
URL(s)   http://www.scripting.com/default.html

Client-side programming

NAME   **COM Technologies**
PROVIDER   Microsoft
DESCRIPTION   The official source for COM based technologies such as
Distributed COM (DCOM), COM+, Microsoft Transaction Server
(MTS), and ActiveX Controls.
URL(s)   http://www.microsoft.com/activex/

NAME   **DOWNLOAD.COM – ActiveX**
PROVIDER   CNET Inc.
DESCRIPTION   Enormous library of ActiveX controls, browsable by category
and keyword searchable.
URL(s)   http://www.download.com/PC/Activex/

NAME Developer.com – Directories
PROVIDER EarthWeb Inc.
DESCRIPTION Host for Gamelan; the official directory for Java, which ha
the biggest collection of Java applets, sorted by application area and key
word searchable.
URL(s) http://www.developer.com/directories/pages/dir.
java.html

NAME Getting Started with Java
PROVIDER Sun Microsystems
DESCRIPTION The place to start learning Java, from the company that orig
nated it.
URL(s) http://java.sun.com/starter.html

NAME Java Technology Home Page
PROVIDER Sun Microsystems
DESCRIPTION The source for Java information.
URL(s) http://java.sun.com/

NAME Java(TM)Boutique
PROVIDER Mecklermedia Corporation
DESCRIPTION Comprehensive Java site, with applet listings, FAQs, news an
more.
URL(s) http://javaboutique.internet.com/

NAME Danny Goodman's JavaScript Pages
PROVIDER Danny Goodman
DESCRIPTION Adjunct to a book. Nice collection of scripts, well document
and explained. Also links to the JavaScript FAQ etc.
URL(s) http://www.dannyg.com/javascript/index.html

NAME JavaScript for the Total Non-Programmer
PROVIDER robyoung@mediaone.net
DESCRIPTION Excellent tutorial, but still a rough ride for the 'total non-pro
grammer'.
URL(s) http://www.Webteacher.com/javatour/

NAME JavaScript Guide

PROVIDER Netscape Corporation

DESCRIPTION The definitive JavaScript reference, from the company that created it.

  URL(s) http://developer.netscape.com/docs/manuals/
  communicator/jsguide4/index.htm

NAME The JavaScript Source

PROVIDER The JavaScript Source

DESCRIPTION Searchable library of JavaScripts. Allows them to be requested by e-mail. Offers a message board.

  URL(s) http://javascriptsource.com/

NAME Live Software: JavaScript Resource Center

PROVIDER Live Software Inc.

DESCRIPTION Collection of example JavaScripts, supplemented by message board support.

  URL(s) http://www.livesoftware.com/jrc/index.html

Keeping up with World Wide Web technology

NAME ADV-HTML Archives

PROVIDER Patrick Douglas Crispen (crispen@netsquirrel.com)

DESCRIPTION Searchable archive of the ADV-HTML mailing list. Excellent way to pick up tips from the professionals.

  URL(s) http://netsquirrel.com/adv-html/

NAME BUILDER.COM

PROVIDER CNET Inc.

DESCRIPTION Excellent site, comprehensive, up to date. Offers an e-mail newsletter.

  URL(s) http://www.builder.com/

NAME DevEdge Online

PROVIDER Netscape Corporation

DESCRIPTION Netscape's site for the Web developer.

  URL(s) http://developer.netscape.com/index.html

NAME   Site Builder Home
PROVIDER Microsoft
DESCRIPTION Microsoft's site for Web developers, based around Site Builder Network magazine. Has a membership program.
    URL(s)   http://www.microsoft.com/sitebuilder/

NAME   developer.com
PROVIDER EarthWeb Inc.
DESCRIPTION Comprehensive coverage of Web technologies, presented in well-organized subsections (reference, classroom, directory, news etc.).
    URL(s)   http://www.developer.com/

NAME   Homepage Now
PROVIDER homepagenow.com
DESCRIPTION Orientated towards the person or business wanting to set up a Web site, it concentrates on supporting the building of that site.
    URL(s)   http://www.homepagenow.com/

NAME   Hotsource HTML Help
PROVIDER Scott Brady (Webmaster@www.sbrady.com)
DESCRIPTION Nifty site with a tight focus on presenting a wide range of practical help for the Web developer.
    URL(s)   http://www.sbrady.com/hotsource/

NAME   Hotwired: Webmonkey
PROVIDER Wired Digital Inc.
DESCRIPTION Rather over-designed site, which is always first with new technologies. Offers an e-mail newsletter.
    URL(s)   http://www.hotwired.com/Webmonkey/
                frontdoor/index.html

NAME   HTML Station
PROVIDER John December (john@december.com)
DESCRIPTION Provided by a respected Internet Web developer, this site is packed with information, especially on the deeper uses of HTML.
    URL(s)   http://www.december.com/html/

NAME **HTML – Welcome from the Mining Co.**
PROVIDER General Internet Inc.
DESCRIPTION Solid attempt to cover HTML and related technologies. Offers a discussion board and chat.
      URL(s) http://html.miningco.com/

NAME **The HTML Writer's Guild**
PROVIDER kynn@hwg.org
DESCRIPTION The HTML Writer's Guild is a large international organization of World Wide Web designers with over 70,000 members in more than 130 nations world-wide. This site is a treasure trove of practical information.
      URL(s) http://www.hwg.org/

NAME **Project Cool**
PROVIDER Project Cool Inc.
DESCRIPTION This site tries to advise on top-flight Web site design, by both looking the part and supplying critical stages in Web design in five steps.
      URL(s) http://www.projectcool.com/

NAME **Techtools**
PROVIDER CMP Media Inc.
DESCRIPTION Plenty of information broken down by category: users, Web developers, designers etc. A great site.
      URL(s) http://www.techWeb.com/tools

NAME **Web Designer's Paradise**
PROVIDER desktopPublishing.com
DESCRIPTION Lots of advice under a simple listing of topics.
      URL(s) http://desktopPublishing.com/Webparadise.html

NAME **Web Developer's Virtual Library**
PROVIDER internet.com
DESCRIPTION Bills itself as the 'comprehensive illustrated encyclopaedia of Web technology' and lives up to that billing. Highly recommended.
      URL(s) http://www.stars.com/

NAME   Web Review

PROVIDER   Songline Studios Inc.

DESCRIPTION   Perhaps the most successful journal format site. Always has interesting and informative content.

   URL(s)   http://webreview.com/wr/pub

NAME   WebDeveloper.com

PROVIDER   Mecklermedia Corporation

DESCRIPTION   Another enormous compendium of information: links organized by general category e.g. Java, JavaScript, Web design etc.

   URL(s)   http://www.webDeveloper.com/

NAME   Webhoo!

PROVIDER   Jonas Nordstrand (jonas.nordstrand@usa.net)

DESCRIPTION   Webhoo offers an extensive Yahoo-like directory of Web developer-related resources and articles. Includes a discussion board.

   URL(s)   http://nordstrand.hypermart.net/webhoo/

NAME   Webmaster resources

PROVIDER   Matt Mickiewicz

DESCRIPTION   Rather plain and simple site that contains a wide range of practical information. Offers an e-mail newsletter.

   URL(s)   http://www.webmaster-resources.com/

NAME   WebReference.com

PROVIDER   Mecklermedia Corporation

DESCRIPTION   Anther gargantuan site, with an emphasis on e-commerce. Offers an e-mail newsletter.

   URL(s)   http://www.webreference.com/

NAME   WebWeavers Page

PROVIDER   Lisa Reid

DESCRIPTION   A list of links (but a very good list) from NASA.

   URL(s)   http://science.nas.nasa.gov/Services/Education/
                Resources/webweavers.html/

NAME   Welcome to Webresource.net

PROVIDER   Webresource.net

DESCRIPTION   Very cleanly organized site, with a practical focus.

   URL(s)   http://www.webresource.net/

NAME   **ZDNet's InternetUser**

PROVIDER   ZDNet

DESCRIPTION   Site that excels in product reviews (of HTML editors etc.).

URL(s)   http://www.zdnet.com/products/internetuser.html

INDEX

Entries which appear in the Resource Guide are shown in *italics*.

OPAC 41, 43, 48–50
  Z39.50 5
Ovid 51, 108

page counters 34
page creation *see* Web page creation
paint packages 17
PDF 25
PERL 22, 62
  CGI Programming FAQ 120
PERL.COM 119
Persistent Uniform Resource
  Locator *see* PURL
Personal Web Pages – Welcome from the
  Mining Co. 79
PICK 52, 110
Platform for Internet Content Selection
  35, 94
Platform for Privacy Preferences (P3P)
  Project 35, 94
Portable Document Format *see*
  PDF
portals 37
PositionAgent 33, 92
Practical Extraction and Reporting
  Language *see* PERL
Professional Presence Network 96
Project Cool 124
publishing *see* Web site publishing
PURL 60
PURL Home Page 117
push publishing 36

Rank This! 33, 92
RDF 60
RealNetworks 83
registration services 33
Report Dead Links to the Major Search
  Engines 91
Resolution on the use of filtering software
  in libraries 55, 111

Resource Description Framework
  see RDF
RGBtoHex 82
Robot Exclusion 33, 92
robot indexing 33
RUDI 52, 110

SALSER 49, 106
scanning 17
Scottish Academic Library Serials
  see SALSER
Scripting news 120
Search Engine Watch 33, 91
search engines 33, 37
SearchZ: the Ultimate Guide to
  Online Marketing, Advertising
  and E-commerce 97
Server Side Includes Tutorial 119
server-side scripting 62–3
servers 7
  Web publishing 29–32
  usage tracking 34
ServerStats.com 90
Sex, Censorship and the Internet 94
SGML 8
SGML/XML Home Page 116
Sharky's Netscape Frames Tutorial 77
Shell International 43, 45, 102
Site Builder Home 123
Site Search Tools 22, 85
SMIL 20, 83
SOSIG 52, 110
South Ayrshire Council: Libraries &
  Information Services 52, 108
Standard Generalized Markup
  Language *see* SGML
Style Guide for Online Hypertext 80
Submit it! 33, 92
SuperJANET 41
Synchronized Multimedia
  Integration Language *see* SMIL